Long Ago When I Was Young

E. Nesbit

Long Ago
When I Was Young

watercolour illustrations by George Buchanan
line drawings by Edward Ardizzone

Introduction by Noel Streatfeild

BEEHIVE BOOKS

Acknowledgement

The poem by C. L. Graves, quoted by
Noel Streatfeild, is reproduced by
kind permission of Punch Publications Limited.

First published 1966 by
Ronald Whiting & Wheaton Limited

This edition first published in Great Britain 1987 by
Beehive Books, an imprint of Macdonald & Company (Publishers) Limited
Greater London House, Hampstead Road, London NW1 7QX

A BPCC plc company

BRITISH LIBRARY CATALOGUING IN PUBLICATION DATA

Nesbit, E.
    Long ago when I was young
    1. Nesbit, E.   2. Authors, English
    Biography
    1. Title
    823'.8   PR419.B4Z
    ISBN 0 356 13274 9

Printed in England

Contents

		page
List of Illustrations		7 and 9
Introduction by Noel Streatfeild		11
CHAPTER 1	*Stuart Plaid*	29
CHAPTER 2	*Long Division*	36
CHAPTER 3	*South with the Swallows*	44
CHAPTER 4	*In the Dark*	50
CHAPTER 5	*The Mummies at Bordeaux*	58
CHAPTER 6	*Lessons in French*	66
CHAPTER 7	*Disillusion*	75
CHAPTER 8	*In Auvergne*	82
CHAPTER 9	*La Haye*	92
CHAPTER 10	*Pirates and Explorers*	99
CHAPTER 11	*At Mademoiselle Fauchet's*	109
CHAPTER 12	*Alfred's Fox*	118

List of Illustrations

COLOUR PLATES

facing page

Among the roots of the copper beech, he showed me two dormice in an old tea caddy 32

He sat down with me on his knee and fed me with bread and milk 49

We took the cat and the doll back to bed with us 64

We got the black pig up to the loft once 81

The old blind, white horse harnessed to the wheel went sleepily round and round 96

We marched gaily into the garden where my mother was entertaining a company of smart friends to tea 113

List of Illustrations

LINE DRAWINGS

	page
When I stepped out at 5 o'clock in the morning	33
Show your hands, Daisy	39
Market stall	47
The fur skin	55
Now I rushed to him	63
I ducked her head first	73
The shepherdess	80
The last stage of the journey	89
There never was such another garden	97
Pirates and explorers, 'The River Nile'	105
A mixture for the patients	114
Body of a big dog fox	123

About this book

E. NESBIT was born in 1858 and she died in 1924. The 'E' stands for Edith but she was always called Daisy. She wrote these reminiscences of her childhood and schooldays long after she was grown up, so by the time she wrote them she was a famous author.

It is puzzling why, with children of her own, E. Nesbit

should look back and write 'Not because my childhood was different from those of others. . . .' From her experience of bringing up her own children, and from studying other people's, she must have known that she had an unusual childhood. From the time she was seven years old until she was twelve she had no settled home. This happens to many children today whose fathers have to move about, but usually some effort is made to give the child a secure background. Nothing of the sort was given to E. Nesbit in those years; she was sent to boarding schools in Brighton in Sussex and in Stamford in Lincolnshire. Then, since both were a failure and the Nesbits were living in France, to a family in Pau who had one little girl. Then, as her family were still in France, to two different schools near Dinan and finally, when she was not yet twelve, to a school in Germany. In one way or another all the schools were ill-chosen for the type of child that E. Nesbit was, and the school in Germany she loathed so violently that, as these reminiscences show, she – the most nervous of children – actually tried to run away from it. It is bad enough for an adult to be alone and friendless in a foreign country; for a little girl of eleven it took courage of a striking order.

Fortunately, though E. Nesbit died in 1924, some of her children lived on long after her and it was from this source that it was possible for her biographers to get an idea of what the little E. Nesbit was like. In these reminiscences she tells herself what a nervous and sensitive child she was, but she was also temperamental. She was one of those mercurial children – and was to be a mercurial grown-up – who is up in the sky at one moment and grovelling as if in the mud the next. William Wordsworth wrote: 'The child is father of the man.' This was so true of E. Nesbit. She was to grow up an intricate, colourful, highly temperamental character. But it is not what E. Nesbit was like as a person that fascinates us today, it is E. Nesbit the author for children. How much of herself and her storm-tossed childhood is in her books?

It is on the whole the opposite side of the picture which comes out in her stories. What these reminiscences show is how rootless, except when she was with her family or when she stayed with Madame Lourdes and Marguerite in Pau, the child was. Perhaps as a result it was as a present to her child self that E. Nesbit gave her fiction families such strong roots. Usually there is a clearly described permanent home. Almost always a closely united family living at home. And, though the wildest adventures take place – some in the everyday world and some in the world of magic – they are almost always shown against a normal family life.

Time is not the same at every age. When a person is a child there is an enormous length of time between one Christmas or one birthday and another. When waiting for a much-looked-forward-to occasion time positively creeps. But time is not like that for grown-ups. Little by little it goes faster and faster until for the old it behaves like a concertina, it closes up until one Christmas is so close to another that it feels as if even while the present Christmas is being enjoyed – the next could be touched with an outstretched hand. E. Nesbit, though as a grown-up writer she could feel time beginning to hurry, never forgot what it was like when time passed slowly. All her books have that plenty-of-time feeling which belongs to being a child. She was helped by the period in which she was writing. In those far-away days children of the class of the children in Nesbit's books were not expected to be anything but children. Nobody ever expected them to help in the house or with the washing up. In the holidays all of every day was theirs to do what they liked with. Perhaps it was the memory of the un-forgettable summer which she and her brothers spent as children at La Haye in France – which she describes so perfectly in these reminiscences – that helped her to write so well about timeless, happy days.

E. Nesbit was a curious writer. It was as if she hugged her characters, both children and magic creatures, to herself saying: 'That's all I'm going to tell you about that lot. Now I'll tell you about something new.' She wrote three books, for instance, about the Bastable children: Dora, Oswald, Dicky, Noel, Alice and H.O., *The Treasure Seekers*, *The Wouldbegoods* and *The New Treasure Seekers*. No fiction children were ever more popular with other children than they were; but when she got to the end of *The New Treasure Seekers* what did she do? She made Oswald, who was supposed to have written the book, write: 'It is the last story the present author means ever to be the author of.' And it was. Plead as children might E. Nesbit never wrote about the Bastables again. It is lucky for us all writers are not like her. Imagine if Conan Doyle had rationed us to three stories about Sherlock Holmes.

Then there was the magic trilogy, *Five Children and It. The Phoenix and the Carpet* and *The Story of the Amulet*. In those books the readers met Robert, Anthea, Jane, Cyril and the baby called The Lamb. But it was not the children who fascinated the public and E. Nesbit had no intention that they should for all her life she loved magic, so it was first the Psammead and then the Phoenix who she placed in the foreground. This was deliberately and carefully done so that she, who created in the Bastables one of the most vivid families in all children's literature, could be sure the children in this trilogy were so faintly drawn that none of us would recognise them if we met them in the street, whereas nobody could in contrast miss either the Psammead or the Phoenix.

The Psammead, when it was first seen in *Five Children and It*, was coming out of the sand yawning and rubbing its eyes. It was a strange creature. 'Its eyes were on long horns like a snail's eyes, and it could move them in and out like telescopes; it had ears like a bat's ears, and its tubby body was shaped like a spider's and covered with thick short fur, and it had hands and feet like a monkey's.' But it was not its appearance that made it immediately popular with everybody who read the book, it was its personality. It was the most contrary beast. 'It isn't talking I mind – as long as you're reasonably civil. But I'm not going to make polite conversation for you. If you talk nicely to me, perhaps I'll answer you and perhaps I won't. Now say something.' What child faced with such a command could find anything to say?

Like all her best creations E. Nesbit knew far more about the Psammead than she told her readers. She had knowledge of its life over thousands of years. As well she knew how it would make out in its future and in the Past. The Psammead was so pawky about its ability to give wishes, yet it was dignified at the same time. It had to grant wishes, like it or not, but it never admitted it, always it hinted that it could refuse a wish if it wanted to. 'You want another wish I expect. But I can't keep on slaving from morning till night giving people their wishes. I must have *some* time to myself.'

All who read *Five Children and It* waited eagerly for the next book about the Psammead but they had to wait, which must have been a disappointment, for E. Nesbit had promised that it would come back. This promise was given at the end of *Five Children and It*. The Psammead, on its way into the Past, heard one of the girls say: 'I hope we shall see you again some day.' Its weak but still dry and husky voice asked: 'Is that a wish?' 'Yes please,' said the girls. Then the Psammead, as it did when it was wish granting, blew itself up before disappearing in the sand.

Although E. Nesbit did not give her readers the Psammead in her next book, two years later she published *The Phoenix and the Carpet* about the same family of children. What a bird was the Phoenix! Its golden egg arrived rolled up in a magic carpet. The children put the egg on the nursery chimney-piece and it would never have hatched out if they had not tried to build a magic fire. The bird, exquisitely beautiful, rose from the flames saying, as it perched on the fender: 'Be careful; I am not nearly cool yet.' Later, when it singed the tablecloth, it said: 'It will come out in the wash.' A startling memory feat for a bird who had last hatched out two thousand years before.

The Psammead had been well educated, but the Phoenix was only superficially brilliant. It covered what it did not know with what it had picked up two thousand years before. It was conceited past bearing, but so beautiful it was hard not to forgive it. Besides, it said some delightful things. 'These wishing creatures know all about each other – they're so clannish; like the Scots you know – all related.'

The Phoenix could not, of course, grant wishes but it didn't have to for there was the magic carpet. It was at its best when all the children plus the cook travelled on this magic carpet to 'a sunny southern shore'. There the natives took a fancy to the cook. 'Excuse me,' said the Phoenix's soft voice . . . ' but I think these brown people want your cook.' 'To – to eat?' whispered Jane. 'Hardly,' rejoined the bird, 'who wants cooks to *eat*? Cooks are *engaged*, not eaten.'

B

The Phoenix, like the Psammead, though vastly popular with E. Nesbit's readers, was allowed to vanish, but alas it vanished for good. It left presents and one golden feather behind it. It departed for ever as it had arrived – in the heart of a magic fire.

Then two years later the Psammead was back. It came in *The Story of the Amulet*. Nothing shows more clearly how hard E. Nesbit tried not to allow the creatures of her imagination to rule her stories than the way she allowed the Psammead to return. She had promised her readers that he would, and she kept that promise, but only in so far as he fitted in with her new interests.

What had happened since *Five Children and It* was that a new influence had come into E. Nesbit's life. She had met Doctor (later Sir) Walter Budge, who was keeper of the Egyptian and Assyrian rooms in the British Museum. This brilliant man had told her about amulets and Words of Power and had interested her in the relativity of time. She was enthralled by all she learnt and bursting to weave her knowledge into a story. But what about the Psammead?

The poor creature reappeared in a most humiliating way. The children found it for sale in a pet shop, where it was called a 'mangy old monkey'. It could not be said to be humbled by its circumstances, nothing could do that to it, but it almost pleaded with the children to get it away.

It is almost certain that E. Nesbit, tingling with excitement at what she had learnt from Dr Budge of real age-old magic, intended the Psammead to play only a small part in the search for the second half of the amulet, but she should have known the creature she had created better than that. From the beginning, even though it could no longer grant the children's wishes, the Psammead stole the story. It utterly refused to be kept in its place. 'You've saved my life and I am not ungrateful – but it doesn't change your nature or mine. You're still very ignorant, and rather silly and I am worth a thousand of you any day of the week.'

If E. Nesbit's readers hoped because the Psammead was back he was going to remain with them they were disappointed. By the end of *The Story of the Amulet* she had finished with amulets and Psammeads. The amulet the children gave away to 'the learned gentleman', who was a thinly disguised Doctor Budge. The Psammead vanished, to live as far as is known for ever, by the great temple of Baalbec.

In these reminiscences E. Nesbit records the happiest months she could remember were those she spent at the house her mother rented in France, which was near St Malo. After her years of wandering, culminating in the much-loathed school in Germany, no doubt that house was not really the dream house she describes. But to her it was perfect because it was a real home with her mother and brothers living in it. She writes that her mother 'With a wisdom for which I shall thank her all my days, allowed us to run wild.'

There is nothing remotely alike about her much-loved holiday home in France and Three Chimneys, the cottage in England in which the children in *The Railway Children* lived, but there is a connection in the reference to running wild. Until the railway children's father was sent to prison they had lived a conventional existence – watched and looked after every moment of the day. The author writes: 'They were just ordinary suburban children and they lived with their Father and Mother in an ordinary red-brick-fronted villa, with coloured glass in the front door, a tiled passage that was called a hall, a bathroom with hot and cold water, electric bells, French windows, and a good deal of white paint, and "every modern convenience" as the house agents say.' But when the children came to live in Three Chimneys all these things vanished. There were no modern conveniences at all, not even running water. But what child cares about such things? What was thrilling for the children was that there was no school and no one to look after them. Mother supported her children just as E. Nesbit had supported hers, by writing, so she had to leave them to their own resources. All of every day was theirs to use exactly as they liked. They had no raft on a pond on which to travel and explore, as had E. Nesbit and her brothers during the summer holiday in France, but they had a railway – and oh what a joy that was.

In *The Railway Children* there is an amusing example of

E. Nesbit's magnificent disregard of facts that she wished to ignore, which is a feature of her books. In the chapter where the children saved the train from being wrecked by a landslide, they stopped the train by waving flags made of the girls' red flannel petticoats. E. Nesbit knew perfectly well that at the date when she wrote the book girls not only did not wear red flannel petticoats but had never even seen one. But when she was a little girl of the age described in these reminiscences she had worn a red flannel petticoat, so since she needed red flannel to make flags she disregarded the fashion and took her children back about thirty years, and if any of her readers thought it odd what did she care, whose creation were the children any way?

Because it was her first and for many years her only home everything to do with Kennington Lane was very clear in E. Nesbit's mind. But in most of her books there is little to show that she must as a child have seen terrible poverty. For though Kennington Lane was a respectable residential street, just round the corner there were slums. But it is possible that one of her best characters, Dickie of *The House of Arden* and *Harding's Luck*, belonged to those days. For little lame Dickie was a cockney child who lived in a slum in Deptford, South East London.

It is almost certain that when E. Nesbit wrote *The House of Arden* she intended to tell a magic story round the two Arden children, Elfrida and Edred. The magic creatures were to be the Warps; there were three of them: the Mouldiwarp who was the badge of the house of Arden, the Mouldiwarp who was the crest, and the Great Mouldiwarp, who belonged to the Ardens' whole coat-of-arms. They were all moles of Sussex origin, though what they spoke was a dialect of their own with no Sussex in it, or at least no modern Sussex dialect, but it could have belonged to the Past for they had been around for centuries. Through the Mouldiwarps Elfrida and Edred by various magical means could visit the Past, and it was in the Past they met Richard, and Richard was Dickie from Deptford. At what moment did E. Nesbit realise that in Richard-cum-Dickie she had found an outstanding character? All that we know for certain is that one year after she had introduced Elfrida and Edred she published *Harding's Luck*, but this time Dickie was the hero.

Dickie, whose story is told in *Harding's Luck*, would have been perhaps one of Nesbit's greatest creations only she was hampered by *The House of Arden*. In *Harding's Luck* she started Dickie's history way back before – in *The House of Arden* – he met his cousins Elfrida and Edred. So, since obviously she could not tell the same story twice, she had to fall back on saying you can read about this in *The House of Arden*. This is not good story telling so that *Harding's Luck*, in spite of Dickie and several other good characters, is not classed as one of Nesbit's best books. But Dickie, both as lame Dickie from Deptford and as Richard Arden in the Past, is one of her best-drawn characters. And what a beautiful end to his story when he throws away today and, being Lord Arden, elects to live in the Past where he is just plain Richard Arden, a man with two good legs who is no longer lame.

Perhaps what stays in the memory longest after reading E. Nesbit's reminiscences is the memory of her fears. She was such an imaginative and often terrified child. How extraordinary then that she should write to frighten other children. Or did she? Was it possible that those frightening Ugly-Wuglies were something imagined when she was a child, and which still haunted her when she was grown-up, so that she had to get them out of her mind by pinning them down on paper?

The Ugly-Wuglies belong to a book called *The Enchanted Castle* first published in 1907. It is a book bursting with rather-difficult-to-understand magic. The children in it are Gerald, Jimmy, Kathleen and Mabel. The Ugly-Wuglies were made by the children to be the audience when they acted *Beauty and the Beast.* 'Their bodies were bolsters and rolled-up blankets, their spines were broom handles, and their arms and leg bones were hockey sticks and umbrellas. Their shoulders were the wooden cross-piece that Mademoiselle used for keeping her jackets in shape; their hands were gloves stuffed out with handkerchiefs; and their faces were the paper masks painted in the afternoon by the untutored brush of Gerald, tied on to the round heads made of the ends of stuffed bolster cases.' These 'things' were placed in the back row of the audience just to fill the chairs. But when Mademoiselle started to clap so did they. 'Their clapping made a dull, padded sound.'

If that was not spine-chilling enough for even a not too imaginative child the 'things' talked in a no-roof-to-their-mouths way through the painted slits Gerald had put in the masks to represent mouths. Worse was to come for the 'things' refused to go away and took on a life of their own. When you come to the part in Nesbit's reminiscences where she suffered from unexplained terrors, try and imagine that child grown up, writing for other children about the truly terrifying Ugly-Wuglies.

When an author dies as E. Nesbit did in 1924 too often their books are forgotten. This did not happen in her case for the books have gone on, loved by generation after generation of children. Not all her books were great but enough of them were for her name to belong forever to literature for children. A poem was published about her when she died, of which this verse should be remembered. It was written by C. L. Graves:

'You pass, but only from the ken
    Of scientists and staticians,
To join HANS CHRISTIAN ANDERSEN,
    The Prince of all the good Magicians.'

There is praise indeed. If only she had been there to read with whose name hers was to be linked.

LONDON 1966   NOEL STREATFEILD.

Long Ago When I Was Young

Not because my childhood was different from that of others, not because I have anything strange to relate, anything new to tell, are these words written. For the other reason rather – that I was a child as other children, that my memories are their memories, as my hopes were their hopes, my dreams their dreams, my fears their fears – I open the book of memory to tear out some pages for you others.

There is nothing here that is not in my most clear and vivid recollection.

When I was a little child I used to pray fervently, tearfully, that when I should be grown up I might never forget what I thought and felt and suffered then.

Let these pages speak for me, and bear witness that I have not forgotten.

E. NESBIT

CHAPTER 1

STUART PLAID

WHEN I was small and teachable my mother was compelled to much travel and change of scene by the illness of my elder sister; and as she liked to have me more or less within reach, I changed schools as a place-hunter changes his politics.

The first school I went to was a Mrs Arthur's – at Brighton. I remember very little about the lessons, because I was only seven years old, but I remember – to my inmost fibre I remember – the play. There was a yard behind the house – no garden, and there I used to play with another small child whose name I have forgotten. But I know that she wore a Stuart plaid frock, and that I detested her.

On the first day of my arrival we were sent into the 'playground' with our toys. Stuart plaid, as I must call her, having no other name, had a battered doll and three scallop-shells. I had a very complete little set of pewter tea-things in a cardboard box.

'Let's change for a bit,' said Stuart plaid.

Mingled politeness and shyness compelled my acquiescence. She took my new tea-things, and I disconsolately nursed the battered torso of her doll. But this grew very wearisome, and I, feeling satisfied that the claims of courtesy had been fully met, protested mildly.

'Now then,' said Stuart plaid, looking up from the tea-things, 'don't be so selfish; besides, they're horrid little stupid tin things. I wouldn't give twopence for them.'

'But I don't want you to give twopence for them; I want them back.'

'Oh, no you don't!'

'Yes I do,' said I, roused by her depreciation of my property, 'and I'll have them too, so there!'

I advanced towards her – I am afraid with some half-formed determination of pulling her hair.

'All right' she said, 'you stand there and I'll put them in the box and give them to you.'

'Promise!'

'Yes, if you don't move.'

She turned her back on me. It took her a very long time to put them in the box. I stood tingling with indignation, and a growing desire to slap her face. Presently she turned.

'You would have them back,' she said, grinning unpleasantly, 'and here they are.'

She put them into my hands. She had bitten every single cup, saucer, and plate into a formless lump!

While I stood speechless with anger and misery, she came close to me and said tauntingly –

"There now! aren't you sorry you didn't let me have them?"

'I'll go home,' I said, struggling between pride and tears.

'Oh, no you won't,' said Stuart plaid, thrusting her mocking face close to mine; 'and if you say a word about it I'll say you did it and pinched me as well. And Mrs Arthur'll believe me, because I'm not a new girl, and you are!'

I turned away without a word, and I never did tell – till now. But I never said another word to Stuart plaid out of school. She tortured me unremittingly. When I had been at school a week or two my paint-box suffered at her hands, but I bore meekly in silence, only seeking to replace my Vandyke brown by mud from the garden. Chinese white I sought to manufacture by a mixture of chalk picked up on the sea-shore, and milk from my mug at tea-time. It was never a successful industry. I remember the hot white streets, and the flies, and Brill's baths, and the Western Road, and the bitter pang of passing, at the end of a long procession, our own house, where always someone might be at the window, and never any one was. I used to go home on Saturdays, and then all bitterness was so swallowed up in the bliss of the home-returning, that I actually forgot the miseries of my school-life; but I was very unhappy there. Mrs Arthur and the big girls were kind enough to me, but Stuart plaid was enough to blight any lot. She blighted mine, and I suppose no prisoner ever hailed the falling of his fetters with the joy I felt when at last, after three or four days of headache and tears, I was wrapped in a blanket and taken home with the measles.

*   *   *

When I got better we went for the mid-summer holidays to a lovely cottage among the beech-woods of Buckinghamshire. I shall never forget the sense of rest and delight that filled my small heart when I slipped out under the rustic porch at five o'clock the first morning, and felt the cool velvet turf under my feet. Brighton pavement had been so hard and hot. Then, instead of the long rows of dazzling houses with their bow windows and green-painted balconies, there were lovely trees, acacias and elms, and a big copper beech. In the school

*Among the roots of the copper beech, he showed me two
dormice in an old tea caddy*   page 34

walks we never had found any flowers but little pink bind-weed,
by the dusty roadside. Here there were royal red roses, and
jasmine, and tall white lilies, and in the hedge by the gate,
sweet-brier and deep-cupped white convolvulus. I think I

When I stepped out at 5 o'clock in the morning.

saw then for the first time how lovely God's good world is, and
ever since then, thank God, I have been seeing it more and
more. That was a happy morning.

The boys – whom I had not seen for ever so long, because of
the measles – were up already. Alfred had a rabbit for me – a

white rabbit with pink eyes – in a hutch he had made himself. And Harry led me to a nook among the roots of the copper beech, where he showed me two dormice in an old tea-caddy.

'You shall go shares in them if you like,' he said.

There was honey in the comb for breakfast, and new-laid eggs and my mother was there in a cool cotton gown pouring out tea, and purring with pleasure at having all her kittens together again. There were cool raspberries on the table too, trimmed with fresh green leaves, and through the window we saw the fruit garden and its promises. That was summer indeed.

After breakfast my mother called me to her – she had some patterns in her hand.

'You must be measured for some new frocks, Daisy,' she said.

'Oh, how nice. What colour?'

'Well, some nice white ones, and this pretty plaid.'

She held up a pattern as she spoke. It was a Stuart plaid.

'Oh, not that!' I cried.

'Not this pretty plaid, darling? Why not?'

If you'll believe me, I could not say why not. And the frock was made, and I wore it, loathing it, till the day when I fell out of the apple-tree, and it broke my fall by catching on a branch. But it saved my life at the expense of its own; and I gave a feast to all the dolls to celebrate its interment in the rag-bag.

I have often wondered what it is that keeps children from

telling their mothers these things – and even now I don't know. I only know that I might have been saved many of these little-big troubles if I had only been able to explain. But I wasn't; and to this day my mother does not know how and why I hated that Stuart plaid frock.

CHAPTER 2

LONG DIVISION

I SPENT a year in the select boarding establishment for young ladies and gentlemen at Stamford, and I venture to think that I should have preferred a penal settlement. Miss Fairfield, whose school it was, was tall and pale and dark, and I thought her as good and beautiful as an angel. I don't know now whether she was really beautiful, but I know she was good. And her mother – dear soul – had a sympathy with small folk in disgrace, which has written her name in gold letters on my heart.

But there was another person in the house, whose name I will not put down. She came continually between me and my adored Miss Fairfield. She had a sort of influence over me which made it impossible for me ever to do anything well while she was near me. Miss Fairfield's health compelled her to leave much to Miss ———, and I was, in consequence, as gloomy a cynic as any child of my age in Lincolnshire. My chief troubles were three – my hair, my hands, and my arithmetic.

My hair was never tidy – I don't know why. Perhaps it runs in the family – for my little daughter's head is just as rough as mine used to be. This got me into continual disgrace. I am sure I tried hard enough to keep it tidy – I brushed it for fruitless hours till my little head was so sore that it hurt me to put my hat on. But it never would look smooth and shiny, like Katie Martin's, nor would it curl prettily like the red locks of Cissy Thomas. It was always a rough, impossible brown mop. I got into a terrible scrape for trying to soften it by an invention of my own. As we all know, Burleigh House is by Stamford Town, and in Burleigh House we children took our daily constitutional. We played under the big oaks there, and were bored to extinction, not because we disliked the park, but because we went there every day at the same hour.

Now Harry Martin (he wore striped stockings and was always losing his handkerchief) suffered from his hair almost as much as I did; so when I unfolded my plan to him one day in the park, he joyfully agreed to help me.

We each gathered a pocketful of acorns, and when we went to wash our hands before dinner, we cut up some of the acorns into little bits, and put them into the doll's bath with some cold water and a little scent that Cissy Thomas gave us, out of a bottle she had bought for twopence at the fair at home.

'This,' I said, 'will be acorn oil – scented acorn oil.'

'Will it?' said Harry doubtfully.

'Yes,' I replied, adding confidently, 'and there is nothing better for the hair.'

But we never had a chance of even seeing whether acorns and water would turn to oil – a miracle which I entirely believed in. The dinner bell rang, and I only had time hastily to conceal the doll's bath at the back of the cupboard where Miss —— kept her dresses. That was Saturday.

Next day we found that Miss ——'s best dress (the blue silk with the Bismarck brown gimp) had slipped from its peg and fallen in to the doll's bath. The dress was ruined, and when Harry Martin and I owned up, as in honour bound – Miss Fairfield was away in London – we were deprived of dinner, and had a long Psalm to learn. I don't know whether punishment affects the hair, but I thought, next morning at prayers, that Harry's tow-crop looked more like hay than ever.

My hands were more compromising to me than anyone would have believed who had ever seen their size, for, in the winter especially, they were never clean. I can see now the little willow-patterned basin of cold hard water, and smell the unpleasant little square of mottled soap with which I was expected to wash them. I don't know how the others managed, but for me

Show your hands, Daisy.

the result was always the same – failure; and when I presented myself at breakfast, trying to hide my red and grubby little paws in my pinafore, Miss —— used to say:

'Show your hands, Daisy – yes, as I thought. Not fit to sit down with young ladies and gentlemen. Breakfast in the school-room for Miss Daisy.'

Then little Miss Daisy would shiveringly betake herself to the cold, bare schoolroom, where the fire had but just been kindled.

I used to sit cowering over the damp sticks with my white mug – mauve spotted it was I remember, and had a brown crack near the handle – on a chair beside me. Sometimes I used to pull a twig from the fire; harpoon my bread-and-butter with it, and hold it to the fire: the warm, pale, greasy result I called toast.

All this happened when Miss Fairfield was laid up with bronchitis. It was at that time, too, that my battle with compound long division began. Now I was not, I think, a very dull child, and always had an indignant sense that I could do sums well enough, if any one would tell me what they meant. But no one did, and day after day the long division sums, hopelessly wrong, disfigured my slate, and were washed off with my tears. Day after day I was sent to bed, my dinner was knocked off, or my breakfast, or my tea. I should literally have starved, I do believe, but for dear Miss Fairfield. She kept my little body going with illicit cakes and plums and the like, and fed my starving little heart with surreptitious kisses and kind words. She would lie in wait for me as I passed down the hall, and in a whisper call me into the store closet. It had a mingled and delicious smell of pickles and tea and oranges and jam, and the one taper Miss Fairfield carried only lighted dimly the delightful mystery of its well-filled shelves. Miss Fairfield used to give me a great lump of cake or a broad slice of bread and jam, and lock me into the dark cupboard until it was eaten. I never taste black-currant jam now without a strong memory of the dark hole of happiness, where I used to wait – my sticky fingers held well away from my pinafore – till Miss Fairfield's heavy step and jingling keys came to release me. Then she would sponge my hands and face and send me away clean, replete, and with a better heart for the eternal conflict with long division.

I fancy that when Miss Fairfield came downstairs again she changed the field of my arithmetical studies; for during the spring I seem to remember a blessed respite from my troubles. It is true that Miss —— was away, staying with friends.

I was very popular at school that term I remember, for I had learned to make dolls' bedsteads out of match-boxes during the holidays, and my eldest sister's Christmas present provided me with magnificent hangings for the same. Imagine a vivid green silk sash, with brilliant butterflies embroidered all over it in coloured silk and gold thread. A long sash, too, from which one could well spare a few inches at a time for up-holstery. I acquired many marbles, and much ginger-bread, and totally eclipsed Cissy Thomas who had enjoyed the fleeting sunshine of popular favour on the insecure basis of paper dolls. Over my memory of this term no long division cast its hateful shade, and the scolding my dear mother gave me when she saw my sash's fair proportions docked to a waistband and a hard knot, with two brief and irregular ends, was so gentle that I endured it with fortitude, and considered my ten weeks of popularity cheaply bought. I went back to school in high spirits with a new set of sashes and some magnificent pieces of silk and lace from my mother's lavendered wardrobe.

But no one wanted dolls' beds any more; and Cissy Thomas had brought back a herbarium; the others all became botanists, and I, after a faint effort to emulate their successes, fell back on my garden.

The seeds I had set in the spring had had a rest during the Easter holidays, and were already sprouting greenly, but alas, I never saw them flower. Long division set in again. Again, day after day, I sat lonely in the schoolroom – now like a furnace, and ate my dry bread and milk and water in the depths of disgrace, with the faux commencements and those revolting sums staring at me from my tear-blotted slate.

Night after night I cried myself to sleep in my bed – whose coarse home-spun sheets were hotter than blankets – because I could not get the anwers right. Even Miss Fairfield, I fancied, began to look coldly on me, and the other children naturally did not care to associate with one so deficient in arithmetic.

One evening as I was sitting as usual sucking the smooth, dark slate pencil, and grieving over my troubles with the heart-broken misery of a child, to whom the present grief looks eternal, I heard a carriage drive up to the door. Our school-room was at the back, and I was too much interested in a visitor – especially one who came at that hour and in a carriage – to be able to bear the suspense of that silent schoolroom, so I cautiously opened its door and crept on hands and knees across the passage and looked down through the bannisters. They were opening the door. It was a lady, and Miss Fairfield came out of the dining-room to meet her. It was a lady in a black moiré antique dress and Paisley shawl of the then mode. It was a lady whose face I could not see, because her back was to the red sunset light; but at that moment she spoke and the next I was clinging round the moiré skirts with my head buried in the Paisley shawl. The world, all upside down, had suddenly righted itself. I, who had faced it alone, now looked out at it from the secure shelter of a moiré screen – for my mother had come to see me.

I did not cry myself to sleep that night, because my head lay on her arm. But even then I could not express how wretched I had been. Only when I heard that my mother was going to the South of France with my sisters, I clung about her neck, and with such insistence implored her not to leave me – not to go without me, that I think I must have expressed my trouble without uttering it, for when, after three delicious days of drives and walks, in which I had always a loving hand to hold, my mother left Stamford, she took me – trembling with a joy like a prisoner reprieved – with her.

And I have never seen – or wished to see Stamford again.

CHAPTER 3

SOUTH WITH THE SWALLOWS

WITH what delicious thrills of anticipation and excitement I packed my doll's clothes on the eve of our journey! I had a little tin trunk with a real padlock; I have it still, by the way, only now it holds old letters and a bunch of violets, and a few other little worthless things that I do not often have the courage to look at nowadays.

It is battered now and the paint is worn off; but then it was fresh and shiny and I packed all the doll's clothes in it with a light heart.

I don't remember anything about our leaving home, or saying good-bye to the boys; so I fancy that they must have gone back to school some time before; but I remember the night passage from Newhaven to Dieppe far too vividly to care to describe it. I was a very worn-out little girl indeed when we reached Rouen and I lay for the first time in a little white French bed.

My mind was, I suppose, a little upset by my soul's sorrows at Stamford and my body's unspeakable discomforts on board the channel boat, and I was seized with a horror of the words Débit de Tabac which I had noticed on our way from the station; I associated them with the gravestone of my father, I don't know why, I can only conjecture that the last syllable of Débit being the same as that of our name, may have had something to do with it. I lay awake in the dark, the light from the oil lamp in the street came through the Persiennes and fell in bright bars on the wall. As I grew drowsier I seemed to read there in letters of fire 'Débit de Tabac'.

Then I fell asleep, and dreamed that my father's ghost came to see me, and implored me to have the horrible French inscription erased from his tomb – 'for I was an Englishman,' he said.

Then I woke, rigid with terror, and finally summoned courage to creep across the corridor to my mother's room and seek refuge in her arms. I am particular to mention this dream because it is the first remembrance I have of any terror of the dead, or of the supernatural. I do not at all know how it had its rise; perhaps in the chatter of some nurse-maid, long forgotten. By-and-by I should like to tell you about some of the things that used to frighten me when I was a child; but just now we are at Rouen where Joan of Arc was burned, and where the church of St Ouen is. Even then the beauty of that marvellous Gothic church filled me with a delight none the less intense for being incomprehensible to me.

We went too, to St Catharine du Mont. The ceiling of the church was blue, with gold stars. I thought it very beautiful. It was very windy on the mount, I remember, and the sky outside was blue, like the church ceiling, with white clouds instead of gold stars.

There was a stall a little way down the hill where a white-coifed woman sold crucifixes and medals and rosaries and pictures. My mother bought me a little painting of the church in an alabaster frame. It was for a long time one of my chief treasures.

We went to Paris. It was very hot and very dusty. It was the Exhibition year. I went to the Exhibition which seemed to me large, empty and very tiring. I saw the Emperor and the pretty Empress driving in a carriage with their little son. The boy was about my own age, and wore a velvet suit and an embroidered frilly collar. The crowd cheered them with wild enthusiasm. Three years later – But this is not a history paper.

The pleasantest part of our stay in Paris was the time my cousin Fred spent with us. He lived in Paris, and knew that

Market stall.

little girls like sweeties. Also he sang the comic songs of the day, *Kafoosleum* and *It's really very unpleasant*, and taught me their long and dreary words. He was very kind to me, and I remember him with tenderness though I have never seen him since. On the whole, though I had a real silver daisy brooch

47

bought at the Exhibition, and more toys than could conveniently be carried in my tin trunk, I was glad to get away from Paris.

As this is not a guide-book I suppose I must not tell you about Tours, and the Convent of Marmoutier. I expected a convent to be a dark and terrible place, with perhaps a nun or two being built into the wall, and I was relieved to find a trim, well-kept garden and a pleasant house, where kindly-faced women in black gowns and white guimps walked about breviary in hand. Nor must I linger at Poitiers, where we saw gloves made, and I, to my intense delight was measured for a small pair of bright blue kid. I liked Poitiers – especially the old Byzantine church now used as a stable. I picked up a bone there, and I treasured it for months. It was human, I was convinced, and I wove many romances round the little brown relic – romances that considerably embittered the reality when I came to know it.

'What's that?' Alfred asked picking the bone from its resting place in cotton-wool in my corner drawer months afterwards.

'A human bone,' I said gravely.

Alfred roared with aggravating laughter.

'It's only half a fowl's back – you little silly.'

Ashamed and confused I flung the bone into the inmost recesses of the drawer, and assured him that he was mistaken. But he wasn't.

We went from Poitiers to Angoulême – how often in school I

*He sat down with me on his knee and fed me with
bread and milk*   page 63

have got into trouble for tracing that route on the map of France when I should have been tracing Cap Gris Nez, or the course of the Rhone! And so, by easy stages we reached Bordeaux.

Bordeaux was en fête – the great annual fair was in progress. The big market-place was covered with booths filled with the most fascinating objects.

I was very happy at Bordeaux until it occurred to some one to take me to see the mummies. After that, 'Farewell the tranquil mind, farewell content.' And here I cannot resist the temptation to put a long parenthesis in my traveller's tale, and to write a little about what used to frighten me when I was little. And then I shall tell you about my first experience of learning French.

CHAPTER 4

IN THE DARK

HOW can I write of it, sitting here in the shifting shade of the lime-trees, with the sunny daisied grass stretching away to the border where the hollyhocks and lilies and columbines are; my ears filled with the soft swish-swish of the gardener's scythe at the other end of the lawn, and the merry little voices of the children away in the meadow?

Only by shutting my eyes and ears to the sweet sounds and sights of summer and the sun can I recall at all for you the dead silences, the frozen terrors of the long, dark nights when I was little, and lonely, and very much afraid.

The first thing I remember that frightened me was running into my father's dressing-room and finding him playing at wild beasts with my brothers. He wore his great fur travelling coat inside out, and his roars were completely convincing. I was borne away screaming, and dreamed of wild beasts for many a long night afterwards.

Then came some nursery charades. I was the high-born orphan, whom gipsies were to steal, and my part was to lie in a cradle, and, at the proper moment, to be carried away shrieking. I understood my part perfectly – I was about three, I suppose – and had rehearsed it more than once. Being carried off in the arms of the gipsy (my favourite sister) was nothing to scream at, I thought, but she told me to scream, and I did it. Unfortunately, however, there had been no dress rehearsals, and when, on the night of the performance the high-born orphan found itself close to a big black bonnet and a hideous mask, it did scream to some purpose, and presently screamed itself into some sort of fit or swoon, was put to bed, and stayed there for many days which passed dreamlike. But that old woman haunted my dreams for years – haunts them still indeed. I tell you I come across her in my dreams to this day. She bends over me and puts her face close to mine, and I wake with a spasm of agonised terror; only now it is not horrible to me to waken 'in the dark'. I draw a few long breaths and as soon as my heart beats a little less wildly I fall asleep again. But a child who wakes from an ugly dream does not fall asleep so quickly. For to a child who is frightened, the darkness and the silence of its lonely room are only a shade less terrible than the wild horrors of dreamland. One used to lie awake in the silence, listening, listening to the pad-pad of one's heart, straining one's ears to make sure that it was not the pad-pad of something else, something unspeakable creeping towards one out of the horrible dense dark. One used to lie quite, quite still, I remember, listening, listening. And when my nurse came to bed and tucked me up, she used to find my pillow wet, and say to the under-nurse:

'Weakness, you know. The precious poppet doesn't seem to get any stronger.'

But my pillow was not wet with tears of weakness. These were the dews of agony and terror.

My nurse – ah, how good she was to me – never went downstairs to supper after she found out my terrors, which she very quickly did. She used to sit in the day nursery with the door open 'a tiny crack', and that light was company, because I knew I had only to call out, and someone who loved me would come and banish fear. But a light without human companionship was worse than darkness, especially a little light. Night-lights, deepening the shadows with their horrid possibilities are a mere refinement of cruelty, and some friends who thought to do me a kindness by leaving the gas burning low gave me one of the most awful nights I ever had.

It was a strange house in Sutherland Gardens – a house with large rooms and heavy hangings – with massive wardrobes and deep ottoman boxes. The immense four-post beds stood out about a yard from the wall, for some 'convenience of sweeping' reason, I believe. Consider the horror of having behind you, as you lie trembling in the chill linen of a strange bed, a dark space, from which, even now, in the black silence something might be stealthily creeping – something which would presently lean over you, in the dark – whose touch you would feel, not knowing whether it were the old woman in the mask or some new terror.

That was the torture of the first night. The next I begged that the gas might be left 'full on'. It was, and I fell asleep in comparative security. But while I slept, came some thrifty soul, and finding the gas 'burning to waste' turned it down. Not out – down.

I awoke in a faint light, and presently sat up in bed to see where it came from, and this is what I saw. A corpse laid out under white draperies, and at its foot a skeleton with luminous skull and outstretched bony arm.

I knew, somewhere far away and deep down, my reason knew that the dead body was a white dress laid on a long ottoman, that the skull was the opal globe of the gas and the arm the pipe of the gas-bracket, but that was not reason's hour. Imagination held sway, and her poor little victim, who was ten years old then, and ought to have known better, sat up in bed hour after hour, with the shadowy void behind her. The dark curtains on each side, and in front that horror.

Next day I went home, which was perhaps a good thing for my brain.

When my father was alive we lived in a big house in Kennington Lane, where he taught young men agriculture and chemistry. My father had a big meadow and garden, and had a sort of small farm there. Fancy a farm in Kennington!

Among the increase that blessed his shed was a two-headed calf. The head and shoulders of this were stuffed, and inspired me with a terror which my brothers increased by pursuing me with the terrible object. But one of my father's pupils to whom I owe that and many other kindnesses, one day seized me under one arm and the two-headed horror under the other, and thus equipped we pursued my brothers. They fled shrieking, and I never feared it again.

In a dank, stone-flagged room where the boots were blacked, and the more unwieldy chemicals housed, there was nailed on the wall the black skin of an emu. That skin, with its wiry black feathers that fluttered dismally in the draught, was no mere bird's skin to me. It hated me, it wished me ill. It was always lurking for me in the dark, ready to rush out at me. It was waiting for me at the top of the flight, while the old woman with the mask stretched skinny hands out to grasp my little legs as I went up the nursery stairs. I never passed the skin without covering my eyes with my hands. From this terror that walked by night I was delivered by Mr Kearns,

The fur skin.

now public analyst for Sheffield. He took me on his shoulder, where I felt quite safe, reluctant but not resisting, to within a couple of yards of the emu.

'Now,' he said, 'will you do what I tell you?'

'Not any nearer,' I said evasively.

'Now you know I won't let it hurt you.'

'Yes.'

'Then will you stroke it, if I do first?'

I didn't want to.

'To please me.'

That argument was conclusive, for I loved him.

Then we approached the black feathers, I clinging desperately to his neck, and sobbing convulsively.

'No – no – no – not any nearer!'

But he was kind and wise, and insisted. His big hand smoothed down the feathers.

'Now, Daisy. You know you promised. Give me your hand.'

I shut my eyes tight, and let him draw my hand down the dusty feathers. Then I opened my eyes a little bit.

'Now you stroke it. Stroke the poor emu.'

I did so.

'Are you afraid now?'

Curiously enough I wasn't. Poor Mr Kearns paid dearly for his kindness. For several weeks I gave him no peace, but insisted on being taken, at all hours of the day and night to 'stroke the poor emu'. So proud is one of a new courage.

After we left Kennington, I seem to have had a period of more ordinary terrors – of dreams from which to awaken was mere relief; not a horror scarcely less than that of the dream itself. I dreamed of cows and dogs, of falling houses, and crumbling precipices. It was not till that night at Rouen that the old horror of the dark came back, deepened by superstitious dread.

But all this time I have not told you about the mummies at Bordeaux. And now there is no room for them here. They must go into the next chapter.

CHAPTER 5

THE MUMMIES AT BORDEAUX

I T WAS because I was tired of churches and picture-galleries, of fairs and markets, of the strange babble of foreign tongues and the thin English of the guide-book, that I begged so hard to be taken to see the mummies. To me the name of a mummy was as a friend's name. As one Englishman travelling across a desert seeks to find another of whom he has heard in that far land, so I sought to meet these mummies who had cousins at home, in the British Museum, in dear, dear England.

My fancy did not paint mummies for me apart from plate-glass cases, camphor, boarded galleries, and kindly curators, and I longed to see them as I longed to see home, and to hear my own tongue spoken about me.

I was consumed by a fever of impatience for the three days which had to go by before the coming of the day on which the treasures might be visited. My sisters, who were to lead me to these delights, believed too that the mummies would be chiefly interesting on account of their association with Bloomsbury.

Well, we went – I in my best blue silk frock, which I insisted on wearing to honour the occasion, holding the hand of my sister and positively skipping with delicious anticipation. There was some delay about keys, during which my excitement was scarcely to be restrained. Then we went through an arched doorway and along a flagged passage, the old man who guided us explaining volubly in French as we went.

'What does he say?''

'He says they are natural mummies.'

'What does that mean?'

'They are not embalmed by man, like the Egyptian ones, but simply by the peculiar earth of the churchyard where they were buried.'

The words did not touch my conception of the glass cases and their good-natured guardian.

The passage began to slope downward. A chill air breathed on our faces, bringing with it a damp earthy smell. Then we came to some narrow stone steps. Our guide spoke again.

'What does he say?'

'We are to be careful, the steps are slippery and mouldy.'

I think even then my expectation still was of a long clean gallery, filled with the white light of a London noon, shed through high skylights on Egyptian treasures. But the stairs were dark, and I held my sister's hand tightly. Down we went, down, down!

'What does he say?'

'We are under the church now; these are the vaults.'

We went along another passage, the damp mouldy smell increasing, and my clasp of my sister's hand grew closer and closer.

We stopped in front of a heavy door barred with iron, and our guide turned a big reluctant key in a lock that grated.

'Les voilà,' he said, throwing open the door and drawing back dramatically.

We were in the room before my sisters had time to see cause for regretting that they had brought me.

The vision of dry boards and white light and glass cases vanished, and in its stead I saw this:

A small vault, as my memory serves me, about fifteen feet square, with an arched roof, from the centre of which hung a lamp that burned with a faint blue light, and made the guide's candle look red and lurid. The floor was flagged like the passages, and was as damp and chill. Round three sides of the room ran a railing, and behind it – standing against the wall, with a ghastly look of life in death – were about two hundred skeletons. Not white clean skeletons, hung on wires, like the one you see at the doctor's, but skeletons with the flesh hardened on their bones, with their long dry hair hanging on each side of their brown faces, where the skin in drying had drawn itself back from their gleaming teeth and empty eye-sockets. Skeletons draped in mouldering shreds of shrouds and grave-clothes, their lean fingers still clothed with dry skin, seemed to reach out towards me. There they stood, men, women and children, knee-deep in loose bones collected from the other vaults of the church, and heaped round them. On the wall near the door I saw the dried body of a little child hung up by its hair.

I don't think I screamed or cried, or even said a word. I think I was paralysed with horror, but I remember presently going back up those stairs, holding tightly to that kindly hand, and not daring to turn my head lest one of those charnel-house faces should peep out at me from some niche in the damp wall.

It must have been late afternoon, and in the hurry of dressing for the table d'hôte my stupor of fright must have passed unnoticed, for the next thing I remember is being alone in a large room, waiting as usual for my supper to be sent up.

For my mother did not approve of late dinners for little people, and I was accustomed to have bread-and-milk while she and my sisters dined.

It was a large room, and very imperfectly lighted by the two wax candles in silver candlesticks. There were two windows and a curtained alcove, where the beds were. Suddenly my blood ran cold. What was behind that curtain? Beds. 'Yes,' whispered something that was I, and yet not I; 'but suppose there are no beds there now. Only mummies, mummies, mummies!'

A sudden noise; I screamed with terror. It was only the door opening to let the waiter in. He was a young waiter, hardly more than a boy, and had always smiled kindly at me when we met, though hitherto our intercourse had not gone farther. Now I rushed to him and flung my arms round him, to his immense amazement and the near ruin of my bread and milk. He spoke no English and I no French, but somehow he managed to understand that I was afraid, and afraid of that curtained alcove.

He set down the bread and milk, and he took me in his arms and together we fetched more candles, and then he drew back the awful curtain, and showed me the beds lying white and quiet. If I could have spoken French I should have said:

'Yes; but how do I know it was all like that just now, before you drew the curtain back?'

As it was I said nothing, only clung to his neck.

I hope he did not get into any trouble that night for neglected duties, for he did not attempt to leave me till my mother came back. He sat down with me on his knee and petted me and sang to me under his breath and fed me with the bread and

Now I rushed to him.

milk, when by-and-by I grew calm enough to take it. All good things be with him wherever he is! I like best to think of him in a little hotel of his own, a quiet little country inn standing back from a straight road bordered with apple trees and poplars. There are wooden benches outside the door, and within a white-washed kitchen, where a plump, rosy-faced woman is busy with many cares – never busy enough, however, to pass the master of the house without a loving word or a loving look. I like to believe that now he has little children of his own, who hold out their arms when he opens the door, and who climb upon his knees clamouring for those same songs which he sang, out of kindness of his boyish heart, to the little frightened English child, such a long, long time ago.

*   *   *

The mummies of Bordeaux were the crowning horror of my childish life; it is to them, I think, more than to any other thing, that I owe nights and nights of anguish and horror, long years of bitterest fear and dread. All the other fears could have been effaced, but the shock of that sight branded it on my brain, and I never forgot it. For many years I could not bring myself to go about any house in the dark, and long after I was a grown woman I was tortured, in the dark watches, by imagination and memory, who rose strong and united, over-powering my will and my reason as utterly as in my baby days.

It was not till I had two little children of my own that I was able to conquer this mortal terror of darkness, and teach imagination her place, under the foot of reason and will.

My children, I resolved, should never know such fear. And to guard them from it I must banish it from my own soul. It was not easy, but it was done. It is banished now, and my babies,

We took the cat and the doll back to bed with us

page 71

thank God, never have known it. It was a dark cloud that over-shadowed my childhood, and I don't believe my mother ever knew how dark it was, for I could not tell anyone the full horror of it while it was over me, and when it had passed I came from under it, as one who has lived long years in an enchanter's castle, where the sun is darkened always, might come forth into the splendour of noontide. Such as one breathes God's sweet air and beholds the free heavens with joyous leaps of heart; but he does not speak soon nor lightly of what befell in the dark, in the evil days, in the Castle of the Enchanter.

CHAPTER 6

LESSONS IN FRENCH

S HE was the most beautiful person in the world. She had brown eyes and pink cheeks, a blue silk dress and a white bonnet with orange-blossoms in it. She had two pairs of shoes and two pairs of stockings, and she had two wigs, a brown and a flaxen one. All her clothes took off and on, and there was a complete change of them.

I saw her first at a bazaar and longed to possess her, but her price was two guineas, and no hope mingled with my longing.

Here let me make a confession, I had never really loved any doll. My affections up to that time had been lavished on a black and white spotted penny rabbit, bought at a Kentish fair; but when I saw Renée it seemed to me that if I could love a doll, this would be the one.

We were at Pau then in a 'select boarding-house'. I was bored with travel, as I believe all children are – so large a part of a child's life is made up of little familiar playthings and objects; it has little of that historic and artistic sense which lends colour and delight to travel. I was tired of wandering about, and glad to think we were to stay in Pau for the winter. The bazaar pleased me. It was got up by the English residents and their fancy-work was the fancy-work of the church bazaars in England, and I felt at home among it, and when my eyes rested on Renée I saw the most delightful object I had seen for many weeks. I looked and longed, and longed and looked, and then suddenly in a moment one of the great good fortunes of my life happened to me. The beautiful doll was put up to be raffled, and my sister won her. I trembled with joy as she and her wardrobe were put into my hands. I took her home. I dressed and undressed her twenty times a day. I made her play the part of heroine in all my favourite stories. I told her fairy-tales and took her to bed with me at night for company, but I never loved her. I have never been able to love a doll in my life.

My mother came to me the next day as I was changing Renée's wig, and said, 'Don't you think it's almost time that you began to have some lessons again; I don't want my little girl to grow up quite ignorant, you wouldn't like that yourself, would you?'

'I don't know,' I said doubtfully, feeling that ignorance in a grown-up state was surely to be preferred to a return to Stamford and long division.

'I am not going to send you to school,' my mother hastened to add, doubtless seeing the cloud that gathered in my face. 'I know a French lady here who has a little girl about your age, and she says that you can go and live with her for a while and learn French.'

'Is she a nice little girl,' I asked. 'What is she like?'

'Well, she's rather like your new doll,' my mother laughed, 'when it has the flaxen wig on. Think how nice it will be to be able to write letters home in French.'

I knew Miss —— could not write letters in French, and the prospect of crushing her with my new literary attainment filled my wicked little heart.

'I should like to go and live with the little girl who is like my new dollie,' I said, 'if you will come and see me every day.'

So I went, my doll's clothes packed in their little tin trunk. And I stood stealing shy side-glances at Marguerite, who was certainly very like my doll, while my mother and her mother were exchanging last civilities. I was so pleased with the new surroundings, the very French interior, the excitement of being received as a member by a real French family, and I forgot to cry till the wheels of my mother's carriage had rolled away from the door.

Then I was left, a little English child without a word of French in the bosom of a French family, and as this came upon me I burst into a flood of tears.

Madame Lourdes could speak no English but she knew the universal language, the language of love and kindness.

She drew me to her ample lap, wiped my eyes, smiled at me and chattered volubly in her own tongue words whose sense was dead to me, but whose tone breathed of tenderness and sympathy. By the time Mlle Lourdes, the only English-speaking member of the family came home from her daily round of teaching, Marguerite and I were unpacking my doll's clothes together and were laughing at our vain efforts to understand each other.

I learned French in three months. All day I was with Madame Lourdes or Marguerite, neither of whom knew a word of English. It was French or silence, and any healthy child would have chosen French, as I did. They were three happy months. I adored Marguerite who was, I think, the typical good child of the French story-books. She wore her hair in a little yellow plait down her back.

I do not think we ever got into wilful mischief. For instance, our starving the cat was quite unintentional. We were playing bandits in a sort of cellar that opened from the triangular courtyard in front of the house and it occurred to us that Mimi would make an excellent captive princess, so we caught her and put her in a hamper at the end of the cellar, and when my mother called to take us home to tea with her we rushed off and left the poor princess still a prisoner. If we hadn't been out that evening we must have been reminded of her existence by the search for her, but Madame Lourdes, failing to find the cat, concluded that she must have run away or met with an accident, and did not mention the matter to us out of consideration for our feelings, so that it was not till two nights later that I started up in bed about midnight and pulled Marguerite's yellow pig-tail wildly.

'Oh, Marguerite,' I cried, 'poor Mimi!' I had to pull at the pig-tail as though it was a bell-rope, and I had pulled three times before I could get Marguerite to understand what was the matter with me. Then she sat up in bed rigid with a great purpose. 'We must go down and fetch her,' she said.

It was winter; the snow was on the ground. Marguerite thoughtfully put on her shoes and her dressing-gown, but I, with some vague recollection of bare-footed pilgrims, and some wild desire to make expiation for my crime, went down barefooted, in my nightgown. The crime of forgetting a cat for three days was well paid for by that expedition. We crept through the house like mice; across the courtyard, thinly sprinkled with snow, and into that awful black yawning cellar where nameless horrors lurked behind each bit of shapeless lumber, ready to leap out upon us as we passed. Marguerite did not share my terrors. She only remarked that it was very cold and that we must make haste. We opened the hamper fully expecting to find the captive dead, and my heart gave a leap of delight when, as we raised the lid, the large white Mimi crept out and began to rub herself against us with joyous purrings. I remember so well the feeling of her soft warm fur against my cold little legs. I caught the cat in my arms, and as I turned to go back to the house my half-frozen foot struck against something on the floor. It felt silky, I picked it up. It was Renée. She also had been a captive princess in our game of bandits. She also had been shut up here all this time, and I had never missed her!

We took the cat and the doll back to bed with us and tried to get warm again. Marguerite was soon asleep, but I lay awake for a long time kissing and crying over the ill-used cat.

I didn't get up again for a fortnight. My bare-footed pilgrimage cost me a frightful cold and the loss of several children's parties to which we had been invited. Marguerite, throughout my illness, behaved like an angel.

I only remember one occasion on which I quarrelled with her – it was on the subject of dress. We were going to a children's party and my best blue silk was put out for me to wear.

'I wish you wouldn't wear that,' said Marguerite hesitatingly, 'it makes my grey cashmere look so old.'

Now I had nothing else to wear but a brown frock which I hated.

'Never mind,' I said hypocritically, 'it's better to be good than smart, everybody says so,' and I put on my blue silk. When I was dressed, I pranced off to the kitchen to show my finery to the cook, and under her admiring eyes executed my best curtsey. It began, of course, by drawing the right foot back; it ended in a tub of clothes and water that was standing just behind me. I floundered out somehow, and my first thought was how funny I must have looked, and in another moment I should have burst out laughing but as I scrambled out, I saw Marguerite in the doorway, smiling triumphantly, and heard her thin little voice say, 'The blue silk can't mock the poor grey cashmere now!'

An impulse of blind fury came upon me. I caught Marguerite by her little shoulders, and before the cook could interfere I had ducked her head-first into the tub of linen. Madame Lourdes behaved beautifully; she appeared on the scene at this moment, and, impartial as ever, she slapped us both, but when she heard from the cook the rights of the story, my sentence was 'bed'. 'But Marguerite', said her mother, 'has been punished enough for an unkind word.'

And Marguerite was indeed sobbing bitterly, while I was dry-eyed and still furious. 'She can't go,' I cried, 'she hasn't got a dress!''

'You have spoilt her dress,' said Madame Lourdes coolly,

'the least you can do is to lend her your brown one.' And that excellent woman actually had the courage to send her own daughter to a party in my dress, an exquisite punishment to us both.

I ducked her head first.

Marguerite came to my bedside that night; she had taken off the brown dress and wore her little flannel dressing-gown.

'You're not cross now, are you?' she said. 'I did beg mother to let you come, and I've not enjoyed myself a bit, and I've brought you this from the party.'

It was a beautiful little model of a coffee-mill made in sugar. My resentment could not withstand this peace-offering. I never quarrelled with Marguerite again, and when my mother sent for me to join her at Bagnères I wept as bitterly at leaving Madame Lourdes as I had done at being left with her.

'Cheer up my darling, my cabbage,' said the dear woman as the tears stood in her own little grey eyes. 'I have an instinct, a presentiment, which tells me we shall meet again.'

But we never have.

CHAPTER 7

DISILLUSION

WAS sent with a servant from Pau to Bagnères. She soon dried my tears by reminding me of the hideous blue and white cuffs which my hot and rebellious fingers had for weeks been busy knitting for my mother, and which I should now be able to present personally. They were of a size suitable to the wrist of a man of about eight feet, and the irregularities at the edge where I had forgotten to slip the stitch were concealed by stiff little ruchings of blue satin ribbon. I thought of them with unspeakable pride.

We reached Bagnères after dark, and my passion of joy at seeing my mother again was heightened by the knowledge that I had so rich a gift to bestow upon her. We had late dinner, in itself an event to me, and then I tasted for the first time the delicious chemin de fer, a kind of open tart made of almond paste and oranges covered with a crisp icing of caramel. I have never tasted this anywhere else, and though I have tried again and again to reproduce it in my own kitchen, I have never obtained even a measure of success. Even to this delicacy the thought of those blue and white cuffs added flavour.

After dinner I slipped away and made hay of the contents of my box till I found the precious treasures. I returned solemnly to the room where my mother was sitting by the bright wood fire with the wax candles on the polished table.

'Mamma,' I said (we called our mothers 'mamma' in the sixties), 'I have made you a present all my very own self, and it's in here.'

'Whatever can it be?' said my mother, affecting an earnest interest. She undid the paper slowly. 'Oh, what beautiful cuffs! Thank you, dear. And did you make them all your very own self?'

My sister also looked at and praised the cuffs, and I went happy to bed. When I was lying between the sheets I heard one of my sisters laughing in the next room. She was talking, and I knew she was speaking of my precious cuffs. 'They would just fit a coal-heaver,' she said.

She never knew that I heard her, but it was years before I forgave that unconscious outrage to my feelings.

Bagnères de Bigorre is built in the midst of mountain streams. Streams cross the roads, streams run between the houses, under the houses, not quiet, placid little streams, such as meander through our English meadows, but violent, angry, rushing, boiling little mountain torrents that thunder along their rocky beds. Sometimes one of these streams is spanned by a dark arch, and a house built over it. What good fortune that one of these houses should have been the one selected by my mother – on quite other grounds, of course – and, oh! the double good fortune. I, even I, was to sleep in the little bedroom actually built on the arch itself that spanned the mountain stream! It was delightful, it was romantic, it was fascinating. I could fancy myself a princess in a tower by the rushing Rhine as I heard the four-foot torrent go thundering along with a noise that would not have disgraced a full-grown river. It had every charm the imagination could desire, but it kept me awake till the small hours of the morning. It was humiliating to have to confess that even romance and a rushing torrent did not compensate for the loss of humdrum, commonplace sleep, but I accepted that humiliation and slept no more in the little room overhanging the torrent.

The next day was, I confess, tiresome to me, and I, in consequence, tiresome to other people; the excitement of coming back to my mother had quickly worn off. My mother was busy letter-writing, so were my sisters. I missed Marguerite, Mimi, even my lessons. There was something terribly un-homelike about the polished floor, the polished wooden furniture, the marble-topped chests of drawers with glass handles, and the cold greyness of the stone-built houses outside. I wandered about the suite of apartments, every now and then rubbing myself like a kitten against my mother's shoulder and murmuring, 'I don't know what to do.' I tried drawing, but the pencil was bad and the paper greasy. I thought of reading, but there was no book there I cared for. It was one of the longest days I ever spent. That evening my sister said to me –

'Daisy, would you like to see a shepherdess, a real live shepherdess?'

Now I had read of shepherdesses in my Contes de Fées. I knew that they wore rose-wreathed Watteau hats, short satin skirts, and flowered silk overdresses, that spinning was part of their daily toil, and that they danced in village festivals, generally at moments when the king's son was riding by to the hunt.

'Oh, I should like to see a shepherdess,' I said. 'But do you mean a real one who keeps sheep and spins and everything?'

'Oh, yes; she stands at her cottage door and spins while she watches her sheep, and eats a beautiful kind of yellow bread made of maize, that looks and tastes like cake. I daresay she would give you some if you asked her.'

The mention of the shepherdess dissipated my boredom. I climbed on my sister's knee and begged for a fairy story. 'And let it be about shepherdesses,' I said.

My sister had a genius for telling fairy-stories. If she would only write them now as she told them then, all the children in England would insist on having her fairy-stories, and none others. She told me a story that had a shepherdess in it and a king's son, of course; a wicked fairy, a dragon and a coach, and many other interesting and delightful characters. I went to bed happy in the knowledge that the fairy-world and this world of ours would touch tomorrow, and touch at the point where I should behold the shepherdess.

I spent the next morning happily enough in drawing fancy portraits of the shepherdess, the king's son, and the wicked fairy. My sister lent me her paints and her best sable brush, and life blossomed anew under the influence of a good night's rest.

In the afternoon we started out to see the shepherdess. Over the cobble stones of the streets, among the little mountain torrents, we picked our way, and came at last to green pastures at the foot of the mountains. The Pyrenees were so bright in their snow coats touched by the sun that our eyes could not bear to look at them.

'We shall soon come to the shepherdess,' said my sister cheerfully. 'You must not expect her to be like the ones in fairy tales, you know.'

'Of course not,' said I; but in my heart I did.

We came presently to a sloping pasture, strewn with fragments of rock.

'There she is,' said my sister, 'sitting on a stone spinning with her sheep round her.'

The shepherdess.

I looked, but could see no one save one old woman, the witch probably.

'Where? I don't see her,' I said. By this time we were close to the old woman.

'There's your shepherdess,' said my sister in English, 'look at her nice quaint dress and spindle and distaff.'

80

We got the black pig up to the loft once
page 100

I looked, but such a sight had no charms for me. Where was my flowered-silk, Watteau-hatted maiden? Where was her crook with the pink ribbons on it? And as for the king's son, his horse could never have ridden up this steep hillside. It was a disenchanted world where I stood gazing sadly at a wrinkled-faced old woman in a blue woollen petticoat and coarse linen apron, a gay-coloured shawl crossed on her breast, a gay-coloured handkerchief knotted round her head. She had wooden shoes, and her crook was a common wooden one with a bit of iron at the end, and not a ribbon nor a flower on it. But she was very kind. She took us up to her little hut among the rocks and gave us milk and maize bread at my sister's request. The maize bread was like sawdust, or a Bath bun of the week before last; but had it been ambrosia, I could not have tasted a second mouthful – my heart was too full. I came home in silence. My sister was sad because the little treat had not pleased me. I did not mean to be ungrateful; I was only struggling savagely with the misery of my first disillusion. Like Mrs Over-the-way I had looked for pink roses, and found only feuilles mortes.

CHAPTER 8

IN AUVERGNE

E WERE to leave Bagnères. Imagine my delight when I found we were to travel not by train, but in an open carriage. In this we were to drive through the mountains, the mysterious snow-clad mountains, into Spain, where the Alhambra was, and oranges and Spanish nuts, and all sorts of delightful things. But alas for my hopes! My brother at home in England chose to have whooping-cough, and so our horses' heads were turned north, and farewell for ever to my visions of Spain.

We drove through lovely country to the other Bagnères, Bagnères de Luchon. On the way we passed a large yellow-stone castle on a hill. Most of the castle was in ruins, but a great square tower, without door or window, still stood as strong and firm as on the day when the last stone was patted into place with the trowel. We wandered round this tower in vain, trying to find a door.

'But it is that there is no door,' said our driver at last; 'within that tower is buried treasure; some day a great wind will blow, and then that tower will fall to the ground, and then the folks of the village will divide the treasure, and become kings of France. It is an old prophecy.'

'But,' suggested my mother, 'has no one tried to get in and see if there really is a treasure?'

The driver crossed himself. 'The saints forbid!' he said; 'who are we that we should interfere with the holy prophecy? Besides, the tower is haunted.'

We could not help wondering how far the ghost and prophecy would have protected that tower from English village boys.

We drove on; presently we stopped at a little wayside shrine with a painted image of St John in it, and a little shell of holy water. At the side of that shrine was a stone with an iron ring in it. Nothing more was needed to convince me that this was the entrance to a subterranean passage, leading to the tower where the treasure was. Imagine the dreams that occupied me for the rest of the drive! If I could creep back at the dead of a night to the shrine – a thing which as a matter of fact I would much rather have died than have attempted – if I should pull up that heavy stone and go down the damp subterranean passage and find the treasure in iron boxes – rubies and diamonds and emeralds, and beautiful gold and silver dishes! Then we should all be very rich for the rest of our lives, and I could send Marguerite a talking doll, that opened and shut its eyes, and a pony-carriage, and each of the boys should have a new paint-box, with real moist colours and as many sable brushes as they liked – twenty each if they wanted them, and I should have a chariot drawn by four tame zebras in red and silver harness, and my mother should have a gold crown, with diamonds, for Sundays, and a silver one, with rubies and emeralds, for every day, and –

I imagine I fell asleep at this point, and awoke to find myself lifted out of the carriage at Bagnères de Luchon.

I didn't go back and lift up the stone with the iron ring, but the dream was a serviceable one, and did duty nobly in idle hours for many a long year; in fact, I come across it unexpectedly sometimes even now.

We spent a day or two at Bagnères de Luchon, and I believe it rained all the time. We drove in a drizzling rain across a rather gloomy country, to see the Cascade d'Enfer. As my memory serves me we crossed a dreary plain and entered a sort of theatre, or semi-circle of high black rocks. In the centre of the horse-shoe, down the face of the rock, ran a thin silver line. This was the Cascade d'Enfer, eminently unimpressive on first view, but when we got out of our carriage and walked across the rough ground, and stood under the heavy shadow of the black cliffs, the thin white line had changed, and grown to a dense body of smoothly-falling water that fell over the cliff's sheer edge, and disappeared like a column of green grass into a circular hole at the foot of the cliff.

'That hole goes down, down,' said our guide, 'no one knows how far, except the good God who made it.'

The water did not fill up the hole; an empty black space, some yards wide, was between us and the falling water. Our guide heaved a lump of rock over the edge.

'You not hear it strike water,' he said, and though we listened for some time, we did not hear it strike anything. That was the horror of it.

We drove on the next day to St Bertrand de Comminges, a little town on a hill with many steeples, whose bells answered each other with sweet jangling voices as we reached its gates in the peace of the evening.

Most of this driving-tour has faded from my mind, but I shall never forget the drive from Aurillac to Murat. We started late in the afternoon, because my sisters wished to see the Auvergne mountains by moonlight. We had a large open carriage, with a sort of rumble behind and a wide box-seat in front. The driver, a blue-bloused ruffian of plausible manners, agreed to take us and our luggage to Murat for a certain price, which I have forgotten. All our luggage was packed on his carriage; we, too, were packed in it, and we started. About five miles from the town the driver halted, and came to the door of the carriage.

'Mesdames,' he said, 'a young relative of mine will join us here, he will sit on the box with me.'

My mother objected, that as we were paying for the carriage, we had a right to refuse to allow his friends to enter it.

'As you will, madame,' he said calmly, 'but if you refuse to accommodate my stepson, a young man of the most high distinction, I shall place you and your boxes in the middle of the road, and leave you planted there.'

Three English ladies and a little girl alone in a strange country, five miles from any town, what could we do? My mother consented. A mile or two further on two blue-bloused figures got up suddenly from their seat by the roadside.

'My father and brother-in-law,' said our driver.

My mother saw that protest was in vain, so these two were stowed in the rumble, and the carriage jolted on more heavily. We now began to be seriously frightened. I know I endured agonies of torture. No doubt these were highwaymen, and at the nearest convenient spot they would stop the carriage and murder us all. In the next few miles two more passengers were added to our number, a cousin and an uncle. All wore blue

86

blouses, and had villainous-looking faces. The uncle, who looked like a porpoise and smelt horribly of brandy, was put inside the carriage with us, because there was now no room left in any other part of the conveyance. The family party laughed and joked in a patois wholly unintelligible to us. I was convinced that they were arranging for the disposal of our property and our bodies after the murder. My mother and sisters were talking in low voices in English.

'If we only get to the half-way house safe,' she said, 'we can appeal to the landlord for protection,' and after a seemingly interminable drive we got to the half-way house.

It was a low, roughly-built, dirty auberge, with an uneven, earthern floor, the ceiling, benches and tables black with age, just the place where travellers are always murdered in Christmas stories. My teeth chattered with terror, but there was a certain pleasure in the excitement all the same. We ordered supper; it was now near midnight, and while it was being prepared, my mother emptied her purse of all, save the money promised to the driver, and a ten-franc piece to pay for our suppers. The rest of the money she put into a canvas bag which hung round her neck, where she always carried her bank-notes. The supper was like something out of a fairy tale. A clean cloth, in itself an incongruous accident in such a place, new milk, new bread, and new honey. When the woman brought in our bill, my mother poured out her woes, and confessed her fear of the driver's intention.

'Nonsense,' said the woman briskly, 'he's the best man in the world – he's my own son! Surely he has a right to give his own relations a lift in his carriage if he likes!'

'But we paid for his carriage; he has no right to put other people in when we are paying for it!'

'Oh, yes, he has!' retorted the woman shortly. 'You paid him so much to take you to Murat, and he will take you to Murat; but there was nothing said about his not taking anyone else, and he says now he won't take you on to Murat unless you pay him double the fare you agreed for, his horses are tired!'

'I should think they were,' muttered my sister, 'considering the number of extra passengers they have dragged.'

My mother emptied her purse on the table. 'You see,' she said, 'here is only the money I promised your son and enough to pay for our suppers; but when we get to Murat I shall find money waiting for me, and I will give him what you ask.'

I believe this conduct of my mother saved us, at any rate from being robbed by violence. The inn stood quite by itself in one of the loneliest spots in the mountains of Auvergne. If they had believed that we were worth robbing, and had chosen to rob us, nothing could have saved us.

We started again. My mother now began to make light of the adventure, and my terror subsided sufficiently for me to be able to note the terrible grandeur of the scenery we passed through. Vast masses of bare, volcanic rock, iron grey in the moonlight, with black chasms and mysterious gorges, each one eloquent of bandits and gnomes, and an absolute stillness, save for the rattle of our carriage, as though, with vegetation, life too had ceased, as though indeed we rode through a land death-still, under the enchantment of some evil magician. The rocks and the mountains beyond them towered higher and higher on

The last stage of the journey.

each side of the road. The strip of flat ground between us and the rocks grew narrower, till presently the road wound between two vast black cliffs, and the strip of sky high up looked bright and blue. The tall cliffs were on either side and presently I saw with dismay that in front of us the dark cliff stretched right across the road. We seemed to be driving straight into the heart of the rock. In another moment, with a crack of the whip and an encouraging word or two, the driver urged his horses to a gallop, and we plunged through a dark archway into pitch darkness, for, with a jolt, the carriage lamps went out. We had just been able to see that we had passed out of the night air into a tunnel cut in the solid rock. Oh, how thankful we were then that the porpoise and all the rest of our driver's relations had been left behind at the half-way house. The driver lighted the lamps again, and explained to us that this was the great arch under the mountains, and to me he added: 'It will be something for you to remember and to tell your children about when you are old,' which was certainly true. That tunnel was unbearably long. As we rattled through its cavernous depths, I could not persuade myself that at any moment our driver's accomplices might not spring out upon us and kill us there and then. Who would ever have known? Oh, the relief of seeing at last a faint pin-prick of light! It grew larger and larger and larger, and at last, through another arch, we rattled out into the moonlight again.

Of course, I shall never know now how many of the terrors of that night were imaginary. It is not pleasant, even now, to think of what might have happened.

At last we reached our journey's end, a miserable, filthy inn, and, with a thankful heart, saw the last of our blue-bloused driver.

The landlady objected very strongly to letting us in, and we objected still more strongly to the accommodation which she at last consented to offer us. The sheets were grey with dirt, and the pillows grimed with the long succession of heads that had lain on them. A fire was the only good thing that we got at Murat. To go to bed was impossible. We sat round the fire waiting for daylight and the first morning train. My mother took me on her knee. I grew warm and very comfortable, and forgot all my troubles. 'Ah,' I said, with sleepy satisfaction, 'this is very nice; it's just like home.'

The contrast between my words and that filthy, squalid inn must have been irresistibly comic, for my mother and sisters laughed till I thought they would never stop. My innocent remark and some bread and milk – the only things clean enough to touch – cheered us all up wonderfully, and in another twenty-four hours my mother and sisters were all saying to each other that perhaps, after all, there had been nothing to be frightened about; but all the same, I don't think any of that party would ever have cared to face another night drive through the mountains of Auvergne.

CHAPTER 9

LA HAYE

AFTER our experience in Auvergne, the rest of our travel was so flat as to have faded almost entirely from my memory. As soon as we reached England, I was sent to school – to a school of which I shall have more to say presently. There were only twenty girls. Miss MacBean was one of the best and kindest women who ever lived – a devoted Christian with a heart large enough to take in all her girls. If I could have been happy at any school I should have been happy there. And I was not actively unhappy, for I lived on my mother's promise that in July I should go back to her again. Where she was I didn't know; but I knew she was looking for a pretty home for us all, I used to write letters to her addressed to St Martin's le Grand, which I think I believed to be in Paris.

At last the news came that she had decided to live at Dinan in Brittany, and that in two short days I was to go by boat and join her. One day passed. The next day at dinner I was hugging myself on the thought of the morrow.

'Tomorrow,' I said to the girl next to me,' I shall be going to my mother in France.'

'Oh, no, dear!' said the governess at the foot of the table. 'Miss MacBean says you're not going till Wednesday.'

With a crash my card-castle came tumbling about my ears. Wednesday might as well have been next year – it seemed so far off. I burst into passionate weeping just as the servant placed a large plate of steaming black-currant pudding before me. I saw through my tears how vexed Miss MacBean looked; she hadn't meant to break the news to me in this way.

'Come, Daisy,' she said after a while, 'don't cry, dear. Have some black-currant pudding – nice black-currant pudding.'

'I don't want any black-currant pudding!' I cried. 'I hate it! I never want any pudding again!' And, with that, I rushed from the room; and from that day to this I have never been able to tolerate black-currant pudding.

Every one was very kind to me; but there was not any one there who could at all understand the agony that that delay cost me. I didn't care to eat, I didn't care to sleep or play or read.

When my mother met me at St Malo on the following Thursday, her first words were, 'Why, how pale and ill the child looks!' My sister suggested that it was the steam-boat, but I don't believe it was. I believe it was the awful shock that came to me over the black-currant pudding.

A long drive on a diligence by miles and miles of straight white road – the fatigue of the journey forgotten in the consciousness that I was going home, not to an hotel, not to a boarding-house, but home.

The small material objects that surround one's daily life have always influenced me deeply. Even as a child I found that in a familiar entourage one could be contented, if not happy; but hotels and boarding-houses and lodgings have always bored me to extinction. Of course, as a matter of theory, one ought to carry one's intellectual atmosphere with one and be independent of surroundings, but, as a matter of practice, it can't be done, at least, by me. I have a cat-like fondness for things I am accustomed to, and I am not singular in this respect. I once knew a woman who, after years of genteel poverty and comfortless economy, had an opportunity of a new life in comparatively affluent circumstances.

'Why ever don't you accept it?' I said when she told me of it.

'I can't make up my mind to it,' she said. 'You see, I should have to leave the furniture.'

I felt sympathy for her, though I hope that in her place I should have been strong-minded enough to make another choice.

At last the diligence drew up at cross-roads, where a cart was waiting, and to this our luggage was transferred. It turned up one of the side roads, and we followed on foot. Up a hill wound the road, a steep wooded slope on one side, and on the other a high, clay bank set with dainty ferns. Here and there a tiny spring trickled down to join the little stream that ran beside the road.

We turned a corner by a farm, through a herd of gaunt pigs nearly as big as donkeys – the sight of which made me clasp my mother's hand more tightly. Each pig had a bar of wood suspended from his neck by a string, so that, if he tried to stray through the hedge, the bar would catch and hold him back. All the pigs tried to walk over this bar as it hung against their fore legs. They never succeeded; but the action gave them all the air of high-stepping carriage-horses.

Then we walked a little further along the white road, and the cart turned in at a wooden gate. We followed along the carriage-drive, which ran along outside the high red wall of the big garden, then through a plantation of huge horse-chestnut trees. To the left, I could see ricks, cows and pigs, all the bustle and colour of a farm-yard.

Two great brown gates swung back on their hinges and we passed through them into the courtyard of the dearest home of my childhood. The courtyard was square. One side was formed by the house; dairy, coach-house and the chicken-house formed the second side; on the third were stable, cow-houses and goat-shed; on the fourth wood-shed, dog-kennel and the great gates by which we had entered. The house itself was an ordinary white-washed, slate-roofed, French country house, with an immense walled fruit garden on the other side of it.

There never was such another garden, there never will be! Peaches, apricots, nectarines, and grapes of all kinds, lined the inside walls; the avenue that ran down the middle of it was of fig trees and standard peach-trees. There were raspberries, cherries and strawberries, and flowers mingling with fruits and vegetables in a confusion the most charming in the world. Along the end of the garden was a great arcade of black, clipped yews, so thick and strong that a child could crawl on the outside of it without falling through. Above the dairy and coach-house was an immense hay-loft, a straw-loft over the stable and cow-house. What play-rooms for wet days! Beyond the chicken-house was the orchard full of twisted grey apple trees, beneath whose boughs in due season the barley grew. Beyond, a network of lanes, fringed with maiden-hair, led away into fairyland.

My brothers eagerly led me round to show me all the treasures

*The old blind, white horse harnessed to the wheel
went sleepily round and round*   page 101

of the new home. There was a swing in the orchard, there were trees full of cherries, white and black.

'And we may eat as many as we like,' said Alfred.

That afternoon we gathered a waste-paper basket full of cherries, and, with strenuous greed, set ourselves to empty it.

There never was such another garden.

We didn't succeed, of course, but the effort, so far as I remember, was attended by no evil consequences. We gave what we couldn't eat to the little black English pig, another of the treasures of the new home.

There was a little black cow, there was a goat who resented with her horns my efforts after goat's milk. I learnt to milk her afterwards though, and she grew very kind and condescending. Then there were two ponies, Punch and Judy, and Punch, my brothers told me proudly, was for us to ride. This was the crowning happiness; we had never had a pony of our own before. He was a tiresome, pig-headed little beast that pony; but we loved him dearly. He had a way of pretending to be frightfully thirsty when you were out riding him, and when, in the kindness of your heart, you let him bend his head to a wayside pond for a drink, he would kick up his wicked little heels and over his head you had to go. If he could rub you off against a tree as you rode across the fields, he would do it with all the pleasure in life. He was rather good at jumping, and he and I had some pleasant cross-country expeditions; but, if anything in the nature of the obstacle you put him at happened to strike his fancy disagreeably, he had a clever way of stopping short at the last moment, when, of course, you went over his head. He threw me three times in this way in one morning; but after that I was up to him.

CHAPTER 10

PIRATES AND EXPLORERS

HAT summer was an ideally happy one. My mother, with a wisdom for which I shall thank her all my days, allowed us to run wild; we were expected to appear at meals with some approach to punctuality, and with hands and faces moderately clean. Sometimes when visitors were expected, we were seized and scrubbed, and clothed, and made to look something like the good little children we were not; then my brothers fidgeted awkwardly on their chairs and tried to conceal their hands and feet, while I nibbled a biscuit or cake in an agony of shyness, not quite unrelieved by a sneaking appreciation of my fine dress, an appreciation for which my brothers would never have forgiven me, had I been foolish enough to show it. But, as a rule, we were left to go our own way, and a very happy way it was. I don't mean that we were neglected; my eldest sister was always a refuge on wet days when a fairy story seemed to be the best thing to be had.

In the midst of all the parties, picnics and gaieties in which our elders were plunged, my other sister found time to read aloud to us, and to receive such confidences as we deemed it wise to make concerning our plans and our plays.

We had gauged the possibilities of the lofts correctly. With trusses of hay or straw, a magnificent fort could be made. I usually held the fort when the boys had built it, and the weakness of the garrison was lessened by the introduction of the two dogs, who defended it with me nobly, understanding perfectly the parts they had to play. We got the black pig up once, but that was a failure. When there was no time to organise a play, when it was not worth while to begin anything because dinner or breakfast would be ready in a few minutes, it was a constant delight to scale the wall behind the stable, and watch the great wooden wheel slowly dragged round the circular stone trough where the apples for cider lay; the old, blind, white horse harnessed to the wheel went sleepily round and round; you could hear the crunch, crunch of the apples as the great wooden wheel went over them, and smell the sweet scent of the crushed fruit as you sat swinging your legs on the wall among the yellow stone-crop and sulphur-coloured snap-dragon; or if you had the time to spare, what rapture to balance yourself on the edge of the stone trough, and walk round it just behind the big wheel, knowing that if you slipped, you might fall on the muddy track outside, but that you were much more likely to fall into the trough itself, in which case your pinafore and stockings (we wore white stockings then) would be richly stained with apple juice to the colour of red rust. If the farmer were in a good temper, he would sometimes take you in to see the apples put in the press; you had to climb up by rough steps cut in the beams if the press was nearly full. At the top, on a little platform, stood the farmer, drawing up the crushed apples from below by bucketsful, and spreading them on their bed of clean straw with a wooden shovel. A layer of straw and a layer of apples, and when the press was full, the big beams screwed down, we hastened below to see the russet juice run out from its stone channel into the great vats.

Though the farm adjoined our house, it was not our property, but as far as we children were concerned, it was just as good as ours, for the farmer allowed us the same privileges that he accorded to his own children; that is to say, if the farmer were in a good temper, we might watch any of the farming operations, if he was not, his own children had to keep out of the way, and so had we.

There was a delightful pond in the field where the farm horses went to drink. It had a trampled muddy shore on one side, and on the other a high bank of yellow clay. We made a raft, of course, out of an old door and two barrels, and successfully sailed across to the yellow cliffs.

'How nice it would be,' I said, 'if there were a cave in these cliffs; we could have no end of a good time and be pirates and things!'

'You don't suppose,' said Alfred scornfully, 'that a pirate chief would wait to find a cave if he wanted one – he would make one of course; I shall make one.'

'I don't believe you can,' said Harry and I in a breath.

'All right,' said my brother, 'you'll see!'

Next morning, when Harry and I went out into the field, there was Alfred, ankle deep in water shovelling out clay from the bank.

'What a big hole you've made,' said I. 'I believe I could get into it if I curled up very much.'

'Ah!' said my brother grimly, 'you thought I couldn't do it.'

'Do you mean to say you aren't going to let us go shares,' said Harry, reading his brother's tone instantly.

'Not a share,' said Alfred firmly, 'this is going to be my cave, and if I find anyone in it without my leave, I'll throw him to the alligators.'

'There aren't any alligators,' said Harry, 'there are only ducks,' and indeed, there were several swimming about the yellow waters of the pond.

'All right,' said Alfred cheerfully, sending a large spadeful of clay splashing into the pond, 'I'll throw you to the ducks then, I daresay they'll do just as well.'

Alfred worked with what seemed to us superhuman vigour, and before evening there really was a hole in the clay bank big enough for him to get into, if, as I said, he curled himself up very much.

'He'll be tired of it tomorrow,' said Harry to me privately, reasoning from his former experience of his brother, 'and then he'll let us have it.' But the next day we found that the roof of the cave had fallen in.

'No one need want to have it now,' I said, but I was mistaken. The landslip, while filling up, had enlarged the hole, so that when the loose clay was cleared out, there was a large enough space for us all to get in, even with the dogs. Alfred twisted some straw into a rope and made it, with string, into a rough mat. This he put at the bottom of his rough cave. I timidly offered to help with this, but my offers were sternly rejected.

'You said I couldn't do it,' he said, 'and I'll jolly well show you I can.'

Harry came to me a little later when I was feeding my rabbits. 'He's got it all so nice,' he said, 'he's roofed it over with a hurdle and he's put a bit of old tarpaulin over it, and he's fastening it down with big stones like the people in the Swiss Family Robinson; I wish he'd let us share in it.'

'Look here,' I said, 'let's walk into town and get him a present then he'll see we're sorry we said he couldn't do it.'

In the broiling sun we walked the five miles into the town and back, returning with a large green sugarstick wrapped in coloured paper which had taken all our halfpennies to buy. With this we approached the pond. Alfred was sitting in his cave with the raft moored at his feet; I waved the sugarstick in the air.

'Look here, Alfred,' I said, 'here's a sucre de pomme for you; we've been all the way to Dinan to get it, and we're sorry we said you couldn't.'

'You little duffers,' he cried, 'I don't want your sucre de pomme, I only wanted you to say you were sorry. You needn't have walked five miles in the broiling sun to do that, you'd like to come over, wouldn't you?' he added, unmooring the raft.

'We really didn't mean to vex you,' I said, as he came across.

'Not another word,' he said handsomely, and rowed us to the cave.

It was a very soft cave, and we had no means of breaking the sucre de pomme, so we took it in turns to suck it; Alfred after some persuasion, consenting to join us in the feast, so as not to hurt our feelings, he said.

That cave was a joy to us for many a day, though there was generally at least half an inch of water in it; and we didn't abandon it till the autumn rains had swelled the pond water, and raised it above the level of our cave.

*   *   *

It was a grand day for us when we first discovered our stream; it was three or four fields from our house, and ran through a beautiful meadow with sloping woods on each side.

Pirates and explorers, 'The River Nile'.

Its bottom was partly of shining sand and stone, and in some places of clay. We built dams and bridges with the clay, we caught fish with butterfly nets in the sandy shadows; we called it the Nile and pretended that there were crocodiles in it, and that the rocks among the woods were temples and pyramids.

One day Alfred proposed that we should try and find the source of it. 'We shall have to travel through a very wild country,' he said, 'explorers always do, and we shall want a good lot of provisions, for I don't suppose we shall get back before dinner-time, so you kids had better sneak as much bread-and-butter as you can at breakfast, and I'll sneak what I can out of the larder, and we'll start directly after breakfast to-morrow.'

We secured a goodly stock of provisions in an old nose-bag which we found in the stables, but it was so heavy that we were glad to hide it under the second hedge that we passed and go on with only what we could carry in our pockets. We struck the river at the usual point.

'I think we ought to wade up,' said Alfred, 'there are no crocodiles in this part of the river, but the lions and tigers on the banks are something awful.'

So we waded up stream, which is tiring work, let me tell you.

'I don't see a single lion,' I said presently, 'but I'm sure I saw a crocodile just now under that bank.'

So we got out and walked by the stream's edge on the short, fine, sun-warmed turf. But presently we came to the end of the field; the stream ran through a wood, and we had to take to wading again, but the water was much shallower and it was easy. We ate some of our provisions, sitting upon a large, flat, moss-covered stone, in the middle of the stream. Then we went on again. Harry began to get rather tired.

'We shall never find the source of the stream,' he said 'I shouldn't wonder if it's thousands of miles away, somewhere up by Paris, I daresay. I vote we turn back.'

But his suggestion was howled down by the exploring party, and we went on. Through a meadow where the flax was drying in stooks, then through another wood we followed the stream, and then with a thrill of delight, we saw that the water ran from a little brick tunnel, the mouth of which was draped in a green veil of maidenhair. I suppose it was about four feet high.

'You'll turn back now,' said Harry triumphantly.

For all answer, Alfred stooped and plunged into the darkness of the little tunnel. I followed, and Harry brought up the rear. It was back-breaking work, but the floor was smooth. If we had had to pick our way, we could never have done it, for Alfred had only a few matches, and lighted one very occasionally.

At last we found ourselves again in the dazzling sunlight, and behold our stream was meandering through a wonderful swamp full of grasses and curious flowers, whose like I have never seen elsewhere. Our stream got narrower and narrower, but we followed it faithfully, and at last, crashing through a hedge, found ourselves in a roadway. Opposite us in the high bank was a little stone basin into which water trickled from above. From this basin a narrow stream of water, not more than a foot wide, ran across the road and under the hedge. This was the source of our stream – this, a wayside well we had passed a thousand times!

We finished our provisions, and knowing now where we were, went home by road. The swamp had coated us with black mud almost from head to foot, and in this condition we marched gaily into the garden where my mother was entertaining a company of rather smart friends to tea.

The sequel was bed.

CHAPTER 11

AT MADEMOISELLE FAUCHET'S

THE happy memories of that golden time crowd thickly upon me. I see again the dewy freshness as of an enchanted world, that greeted us when we stole down carrying our shoes in our hands long before the rest of the household was astir. I smell the scents of dead leaves and wood smoke, and it brings back to me the bonfires on autumn evenings when we used to play at Red Indians and sit round the fire telling stories, and when that palled, dig out from the grey and red ashes the potatoes we had put there to roast, and eat the half-cooked, blackened, smoke-flavoured dainties with keenest appreciation; the rare days when we went to Dinard and paddled in the shallow waters of the bay between blue sky and gold sand, picking limpets from the rocks and wishing for wooden spades, which Dinard then, at least, did not produce.

A part of the infinite charm of those days lies in the fact that we were never bored, and children are bored much more often and much more deeply than their elders suppose.

I remember an occasion when some well-meaning friends persuaded my mother that my education was being neglected. I was sent to a select French school, Mademoiselle Fauchet's in Dinan, but owing to some misunderstanding I arrived five days before the other girls. Mademoiselle Fauchet kindly consented to overlook the mistake and keep me till the other girls arrived. I had a paint-box which pleased me for the first day, but the boredom of the other four days is branded on my memory in grey letters. Mademoiselle Fauchet was busy in visiting her friends and receiving them. She took me out for a serious walk every day. We walked for an hour, and then Mademoiselle Fauchet returned to her visiting and I to the bare schoolroom. I had brought a few books with me and these I devoured in an hour or two. There were no books in the schoolroom but lesson-books, thumbed, dog's eared and ink-stained. There was no one to talk to save the severe cook, who was kind to me in her way but didn't understand children.

There was a grey-walled garden full of fruit that I must not touch, and a locked book-case in Mademoiselle Fauchet's salon, full of books that I must not read.

I was not conscious of being unhappy, only bored, bored to extinction. On the fourth day I persuaded Mademoiselle Fauchet to vary our prim walk round the town. She asked me where I would like to go, and I said La Fontaine.

Mademoiselle Fauchet meant to be kind according to her lights, but she was the ideal schoolmistress, grey-haired, prim, bloodless; however, she conceded this to me and I was grateful. We started for La Fontaine.

La Fontaine is one of the show places of Dinan, as it has a natural fountain of mineral water. There is a casino where balls and fêtes and merry-makings are held, where bands play and little coloured lamps glimmer in the trees. All this awakened no associations, stirred nothing in me, for I had never been to a fête at La Fontaine, but below the platform on which the casino was built, ran a stream, our stream, our Nile, on its way to join the river ———. The sight of it was too much for me. I remembered our happy exploring parties, the muddy dams we had built across it; I thought of the rabbits and the garden at home, and my brothers and my mother, and in the midst of one of mademoiselle's platitudes on the beauty of the scene, I began to run. Mademoiselle Fauchet called after me, she even ran a little I believe, but the legs of fifty years are not a match for the legs of ten. I ran faster and faster down the avenue of chestnuts. I reached our meadow where the stream ran just the same as in the days when I was free to make a paradise of it. I ran on and on, up the slope over the cornfield, across the road, through our own meadow, and never stopped until I flung myself into my sister's arms. Then, and not till then, the fact dawned upon me that I had run away from school. I don't recall the explanations that must have followed on my return. I know that I cried a great deal, and felt that I had committed an awful crime. I couldn't explain my feelings to myself, but I knew that in the same circumstances I should have done the same again, though I wept heartfelt tears of penitence for having done it at all. I think my mother must have understood something of what I went through, for she did not send me back.

Another period of acute boredom came to me some years later when I went to stay with some friends of my mother's in the north of London. They lived in a dreary square apart from the main thoroughfare, so that if you looked out over the brown wire blinds you never saw anything pass but butchers' and bakers' carts. If I went for a walk, the sordid ugliness of Islington outraged the feelings of a child who had always found her greatest pleasures and life's greatest beauties in the green country. The people with whom I was staying were the kindest hearted people in the world; they would have done anything to please me if they had only known what I wanted, but they didn't know, that was just it.

*We marched gaily into the garden where my mother was entertaining
a company of smart friends to tea*   page 108

The dining-room was mahogany and leather with two books in it, the Bible and Family Prayers. They stood on the sideboard, flanked on one side by a terra-cotta water-bottle oozing sad tears all day into a terra-cotta saucer, and on the other by a tea-caddy. Upstairs in the drawing-room, which was only used on Sundays, were a few illustrated gift-books, albums, and types of beauty arranged on a polished, oval, walnut centre table. The piano was kept locked. There were a few old bound volumes of *Good Words*, which I had read again and again.

The Master of the house, a doctor, was, my mother tells me, a man of brains, but I only saw him at meals and then he seldom spoke. The lady of the house had a heart full of kindness, and a mind full of court circular, she talked of nothing else. Her daughters were kind to me in their way, and the games I had with them were my only relaxation. The doctor talked very occasionally of his patients, and this interested me. One night I went into the surgery and found the bottles of medicine which his assistants had made up, standing in a row waiting for their white paper wrappings. I didn't in the least realise what I was doing when I thought to escape from my boredom by mixing the contents of these bottles in a large jug; and then in partially filling up the bottles again with the mixture. When I had filled and corked them all, I slipped away; it was done in pure mischief and with no thought of consequences; but when I woke that night in bed and suddenly

remembered that I had heard that medicines that were given
for some complaints were bad for others, and absolutely harm-
ful, my heart stood still. Suppose some poor sick person died,

A mixture for the patients.

whom Dr —— would have cured, because I had mixed up
his medicine with something else. I fully resolved to own up
next morning, but the next morning I reflected that perhaps
some of the people that had taken my mixture might die of it
and then I should be hanged for murder; it seemed to me

wiser to wait and see what happened. If any one did die, and Dr —— were accused of poisoning his patients, I would come forward in the court of justice, as people did in the books, and own that I, and I alone, had been to blame, making my confession among the sympathetic tears of usher and jury, the judge himself not remaining dry-eyed. This scene so much appealed to me that I almost forgot that before it could be enacted somebody would have to die of my mixture. When I remembered this I wept in secret; when I thought of the scene in which I should nobly own my guilt, I secretly exulted. I was not bored now. Whatever else might be the effect of my mixtures, they had certainly cured my boredom. Day after day passed by in spasms of alternate remorse and day-dreaming; every day I expected Dr —— to announce at dinner that some of his patients had breathed their last in inexplicable circumstances, but he never said anything of the kind, and when a week had passed, I was convinced that so good a doctor never gave anybody any medicine that could do them any harm in any condition, and that one of his medicines was as good for any complaint as any others. Whether this was so, or whether someone had been a witness of my act in the surgery, and had re-made the mixtures, I shall never know, but in the reaction following my anxiety, boredom settled down upon me more heavily than ever. I wrote a frantic letter to my mother begging her to take me away, for I was so miserable, I wished I was dead. Not having any stamps, I gave this letter to

Mrs —— to post. I don't suppose she thought she was doing any harm when she opened and read it, and I hope she was gratified by its contents. She added a note to my mother begging her to accede to my request, and to take me away at once. It was years before I forgave her for reading that letter, and to this day I am afraid she has never forgiven me for writing it.

My mother was at Penhurst at the time; I was sent down to her in deep disgrace, and my mother received me with gentle reproaches that cut me to the heart. My sister was exceedingly angry with me, perhaps with some cause, and pointed out to me how ungrateful it was to repay Mrs —— by writing such a letter. I defended myself stoutly.

'I wrote it for Mamma and not for her,' and though I was sorry for having hurt the feelings of one I knew had tried to be kind to me, yet I fear the verdict of my unregenerate heart was 'serve her right'. I felt that I was being unjustly blamed, and though I was sorry I would not say so, and the next morning I wandered up through Penshurst church-yard, and through a little wicket-gate into the park, where the splendour of a blaze of buttercups burst upon me. The may-trees were silver-white, the skylarks singing overhead; I sat down under a white may-tree. The spirit of the spring breathed softly round me, and when I got up to go back I was in love and charity with all men and all women except Mrs ——.

'I am sorry if I have been naughty,' I said to my sister; 'I didn't mean to be, but –'

'That will do,' she said, skilfully stopping my confidences, 'now I do hope you are going to try and be a good girl, and not make dear Mamma unhappy.'

'I will be good,' I said; 'oh, I will indeed!' And as long as I stayed among the golden buttercups and silver may-bushes, I believe I was moderately good.

CHAPTER 12

ALFRED'S FOX

W HEN I began to write of the recollections of my childhood, I thought that all those days which I remember could well be told in these twelve chapters. But the remembrances of that long ago time crowded thickly on me, and I wandered in the pleasant fields of memory, where time ceases to be. So my twelfth chapter is reached, and finds me still only ten years old, and finds me, moreover, with not one-tenth of the events of those ten years recorded. If only one's memory were as good for the events of yesterday – of last week, of last year!

I have left myself no space to tell you of my adventures in Germany and France during the war of 1870, of my English schooldays, of much that is not ever to be forgotten by me. Since I must needs choose one out of many remembrances, I choose my Kentish home, dearer to me than all. After many wanderings my mother took a house at Halstead, 'The Hall', it was called, but the house itself did not lend itself to the pretensions of its name. A long, low, red-brick house, that might have been commonplace but for the roses and ivy that clung to the front of it, and the rich, heavy jasmine that covered the side. There was a smooth lawn with chestnut trees round it, and a big garden, where flowers and fruit and vegetables grew together, as they should, without jealousy or class-distinction. There never were such peonies as grew among our currant-bushes, nor such apricots as hung among the leaves on the sunny south wall. From a laburnum-tree in a corner of the lawn we children slung an improvised hammock, and there I used to read and dream, and watch the swaying green gold of leaf and blossom.

Our garden ran round three sides of a big pond. Perhaps it was true that the pond did not make the house more healthy. It certainly made it more interesting. Besides the raft (which was but a dull thing when the boys were away at school), there were nooks among the laburnums and lilacs that grew thickly round the pond, nooks where one could hide with one's favourite books, and be secure from the insistent and irritating demands so often made on one's time by one's elders. For grown-up people never thought of spoiling their clothes by penetrating the shrubbery. Here, on many a sunny day, have I lounged away the morning, stifling conscience with Mrs Ewing's tales, and refusing to remember the tangle of untidiness in which I had left my room involved.

For I had a little room of my own, a little, little room, with a long low window and a window-ledge, where bright plants in pots, encouraged by the western sun, withstood the inter-mittence of my attentions, and blossomed profusely. My book-case stood by this window, an old mahogany bookcase with a deep top drawer that let down to form a writing-table. Here I used to sit and write – verse, verse, always verse – and dream of the days when I should be a great poet, like Shakespeare, or Christina Rossetti! Ah me! that day was long in coming! But I never doubted then that it would come.

Here I wrote and dreamed, and never showed my verses or told my dreams for many a long month. But when I was fifteen I ventured to show some verses to my mother. She showed them to Mr Japp, then editor of *Good Words* and the *Sunday Magazine*, and never shall I forget the rapture of delight and of gratitude with which I received the news that my verses had been accepted. By-and-by they were printed, and I got a cheque for a guinea – a whole guinea, think of it! Now the day when I should be a poet seemed almost at hand. Had I not had a poem printed?

Besides the desk and the well-oiled key, that formed so excellent a defence against 'the boys' – for what young poet could ever set down a line with the possibility of even the best-loved brothers looking over her shoulder? – my little room had another feature, by turns a terror and a charm. A little trap-door in the ceiling led to that mysterious and delightful region between the roof and the beams, a dark passage leading all round the house, and leading too – oh, deep and abiding joy! – to a little door that opened on the roof itself. This, until the higher powers discovered it, was a safer haven even than the shrubbery. Enclosed by four pointed roofs of tiles was a central space – safe, secluded – whence one could see the world around, oneself invisible, or at least unseen. Another trap-door, from the linen-closet by the boys' bedroom, afforded them an equal access to this same paradise. We kept a store of books and good things in the hollow of the roof, and many a pleasant picnic have we enjoyed there. Happy, vanished days, when to be on the roof and to eat tinned pineapple in secret con-stituted happiness!

It was an uneventful, peaceful, pleasant time. The only really exciting thing was the presence, within a stone's throw of our house, of our landlady's son, who lived all alone in a little cottage, standing in the fields. He was reported mad by the world, eccentric by his friends; but, as we found him, perfectly harmless. His one delusion, as far as I know, was that he was the rightful owner, nay, more, the rightful tenant of our house, and about once in six months he used to terrify the whole household by appearing with a carpet bag at the front door and announcing that he had come to take possession. This used to alarm us all very much, because if a gentleman is eccentric enough to wish to 'take possession' of another person's house, there is no knowing what he may be eccentric enough to do next. But he was always persuaded to go away peaceably, and I don't think we need have been so frightened. Once while he was in the drawing-room being persuaded by my mother I peeped into the carpet bag he had left in the hall. It contained three empty bottles that had held mixed pickles, a loaf of bread and a barrister's wig and gown.

Poor gentleman, I am afraid he was very eccentric indeed.

Did I say that his existence was our only excitement? Is it possible that I have forgotten the dreadful day when my brother Alfred shot a fox?

He drew me mysteriously aside one morning after breakfast.

'Daisy,' he said, 'can you keep a secret?'

I could, I asseverated.

He drew me into his room, locked the door, and then opening a cupboard displayed the body of a big dog-fox.

'Where did you get it?'

'I shot it.'

'Oh, poor thing.'

'Poor thing indeed,' repeated my brother indignantly. 'Don't you know no one would ever speak to me again if they knew I had shot a fox?'

Body of a big dog fox.

'Then why did you?' was the natural rejoinder.

'I didn't mean to. I was out this morning after wood pigeons, and I saw something move in the bushes. I thought it was a rabbit and fired, and it was *this*. What shall I do with it?'

'Bury it, we can have a splendid funeral,' I said.

'You baby!'

I was constantly forgetting that Alfred, at seventeen, was grown-up, and that our old games no longer interested him.

'Well stuff it, then.'

You will hardly believe it, but we really did try to stuff that fox. My brother skinned it, skilfully enough, and we buried the body. We bought a shilling book on taxidermy. We spent many shillings on chemicals; we nailed the fox's skin to the inside of the cupboard door and operated on it. My interest in the process was not lessened by the fact that I felt that the fox when stuffed must be kept from all eyes but our own hidden for ever in the depths of that cupboard, lest the world in general should find out that Alfred had shot a fox, and that I had been an accessory after the fact, and should so decline 'ever to speak to us again.'

But we never stuffed it. We never even succeeded in curing the skin, which after a while cried aloud for vengeance so unmistakably that we had to take it out and bury it secretly beside the body it had covered.

Both interments were conducted in the very early morning before even the maids were stirring, when the dew was grey on the grass, and the scent of the wet earth was sweet and fresh.

When all the fox was buried I breathed more freely. Perhaps no one would ever know, and people would go on 'speaking to us'.

I remember after the burial of the skin we went for a walk

through the long wet grass, and came home with wet feet and happy hearts.

Oh, those dewy mornings – the resurrection of light and life in the woods and fields! Would that it were possible for all children to live in the country where they may drink in, consciously or unconsciously, the dear delights of green meadow and dappled woodland! The delight in green things growing, in the tender beauty of the evening light on grey pastures, the glorious splendour of the noonday sun on meadows golden with buttercups, the browns and purples of winter woodlands – this is a delight that grows with one's growth – a delight that 'age cannot wither nor custom stale', a delight that the years who take from us so much can never take away – can but intensify and make more keen and precious.

> 'Nature never did betray
> The heart that loved her.'

My book of memory lies open always at the page where are the pictures of Kentish cherry orchards, field and farm and gold-dim woodlands starred with primroses, light copses where the blue-bells and wind-flowers grow. Yes, blue-bells and wind-flowers to me and to all who love them. Botanists who pull the poor, pretty things to pieces may call them hyacinths and anemones.

And most plainly of all, among the dream pictures shows our old garden at home.

There is a grey-walled garden far away
　From noise and smoke of cities where the hours
　Pass with soft wings among the happy flowers
And lovely leisure blossoms every day.

There, tall and white, the sceptral lily blows;
　There grow the pansy pink and columbine,
　Brave holly-hocks and star-white jessamine
And the red glory of the royal rose.

There greeny glow-worms gem the dusky lawn,
　The lime-trees breathe their fragrance to the night,
　Pink roses sleep, and dream that they are white
Until they wake to colour with the dawn.

There in the splendour of the sultry noon
　The sunshine sleeps upon the garden bed,
　Where the white poppy droops a drowsy head
And dreams of kisses from the white full moon.

*　　*　　*

And there, all day, my heart goes wandering,
　Because there first my heart began to know
　The glories of the summer and the snow,
The loveliness of harvest and of spring.

126

There may be fairer gardens – but I know
    There is no other garden half so dear
    Because 'tis there, this many, many a year,
The sacred sweet white flowers of memory grow.